Bali

Front cover: traditional Balinese boat

Right: Barong dancer

TOP 10 ATTRACTIONS

Tanah Lot • This dramatic, wave-lashed sea temple is the most photographed sight in Bali, especially at sunset *(page 72)*

Rice terraces • A distinctive feature of Bali, they can be found all over the island, perhaps most impressively at Jatiluwih *(page 72)*

Bukit beaches •
The golden and white-sand surf beaches and coves of the Bukit Peninsula are the most beautiful in Bali *(page 33)*

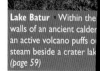

Lake Batur • Within the walls of an ancient caldera an active volcano puffs out steam beside a crater lake *(page 59)*

Petulu • Every evening at sunset, thousands of white Javan pond herons and plumed egrets come in to land and roost for the night in the treetops (page 45)

Tenganan • A 700-year-old walled village where the residents practise a time-honoured lifestyle based around ritual and ceremony (page 55)

Art in Ubud • Fine Balinese art can be found in the Museum Puri Lukisan and the Neka Art Museum (page 42)

The Gili Islands • Sprinkled off the northwest shore of Lombok are three tiny emerald islands, floating in a turquoise sea (page 76)

Bedugul • This market village rests in the mountains close to a trio of sparkling lakes (page 63)

Kecak Dance • Bali's most spectacular choreographic performance involves a chorus of bare-chested men (page 91)

A PERFECT DAY

9.00am **Breakfast**

Start the day in Ubud by having breakfast at Café Lotus with its romantic outlook over the beautiful pink-flowering lotus pond of Pura Taman Sariswati – a temple dedicated to the goddess of learning, wisdom and the arts.

11.00am **Art and other distractions**

Visit the Neka Art Museum, which presents an exceptional collection of artwork by many famous Balinese and Indonesian artists as well as foreign artists who have lived in Bali and influenced the local art movement. Alternatively, wander through the Sacred Monkey Forest and observe the behaviour of the mischievous, long-tailed grey macaques.

12.30pm **Rural idyll**

Enjoy a picturesque 20-minute walk through the rice fields along the Abangan waterway to Sari Organic for lunch. This simple warung serves delicious vegetarian dishes with ingredients harvested from the on-site organic farm. The views from here are stunning.

10.00am **Browsing**

Browse the handicrafts in Ubud market. The narrow, crowded alleyways are crammed with paintings, wooden artefacts such as windchimes, batik quilts and much more, stretching in all directions. Bargaining is part of the fun.

IN BALI

3.30pm Spa treatment

Upon arrival in Seminyak, you can either explore the designer boutiques or be pampered at Prana Spa, which is fashioned after a sumptuous 16th-century Indian palace (book in advance). Some of the treatments and rituals here have their origins in the Majapahit Royal Courts of Java, while others are Ayurvedic – from ancient India.

10.00pm Nightlife

Experience the island's best nightlife scene through Seminyak's wide choice of cocktail lounges, live music bars and nightclubs that pump till dawn.

6.00pm Cocktails

Head to the famous and fashionable Ku De Ta, beach club, restaurant and party venue. This is *the* place to see and be seen at sunset for a passionfruit and vanilla highball cocktail against a backdrop of spectacular red skies, crashing ocean waves and coastline views.

2.00pm Heading south

Take the one-hour drive down to trendy Seminyak, stopping en route at the woodcarving village of Mas. Here, shops and galleries line the main street, but if you wander into the back lanes you will see the artisans at work.

8.00pm Dinner

Relish an unforgettable dinner in chic surroundings at Sarong Restaurant (advance reservation essential), where you will be served a fine dining twist on the street foods of China, Thailand, Malaysia and India.

CONTENTS

71

86

13

INTRODUCTION

Bali is a place that dreams are made of: a volcanic island, of terraced, emerald rice fields; tropical forests of fragrant clove and cinnamon trees strewn with flowers; a magical, delicate culture of music, art, dance, daily rituals and exotic temples, all surrounded by a warm, silken sea. Perhaps the island's greatest treasure is its people – charming, endlessly gracious, and mysteriously able to balance a 21st-century world of internet cafés and motorcycles with ancient traditions and a unique spirituality. Bali is sometimes confused with James Michener's fictional South Pacific island of Bali Hai (which would have been thousands of miles to the east); however, Bali itself is very Asian, was never host to American soldiers during World War II and is more amazing than anything you'd find in a novel.

Climate

Bali's tropical climate is hot and humid all year. There is a dry season (June to September) and a wet season (December to March); intermediate months vary.

Lying to the east of Java and with an area of 5,623 sq km (2,171 sq miles), Bali is one of the smaller islands in the vast Indonesian archipelago but it is the most important tourism destination in this island nation of 225 million people. The Balinese are overwhelmingly Hindu, a miraculously flourishing remnant of the ancient Hindu kingdoms that once dominated Java and other parts of the region. Unique amidst the 95 percent Muslim population of the rest of Indonesia, Bali is a world unto itself and an island of tranquillity despite the political instability other areas of the nation have experienced in recent years.

Rice terraces are a feature of the Balinese interior

Bali is not the untouched paradise of the 1920s and 1930s, when anthropologist Margaret Mead studied the gentle, mysterious Balinese personality, and a few daring adventurers and celebrities such as Charlie Chaplin and Noel Coward frolicked in rivers and pools in the forests outside Ubud. In the heavily developed southern part of the island, you will find only traces of the idyllic, low-budget, hippie-style mecca that developed in the 1960s and early 1970s. At that time, Kuta consisted of swamps, farms and a few simple thatch-roof hotels beside the sea; today, it is a frenetic, motorcycle-filled, thoroughly international town of endless hotels, restaurants, bars, tourist markets and sleek, elegant shops. Ubud, which was a mere village of footpaths, temples and rice fields, has become the island's cultural and artistic centre; its countryside is dotted with some of the most beautiful rustic resorts in the world. But in the mist-covered mountains, on the northern coast, and

Naming Names

Why do many Balinese seem to have the same names?

In sudra or jaba (commoner) families, the first-born is called Wayan, Putu or Gede; the second Made or Nengah; the third Nyoman or Komang; the fourth Ketut. Then the list starts over again, so the fifth (or rarely ninth) is another Wayan, sixth Made and so on. A male is prefixed by I (pronounced 'Ee'); a female by Ni.

Wesia (merchant class) use Gusti Ngurah for a man, Gusti Ayu for a woman. Among the kasatria (nobility) the titles are Cokorda, Dewa or Anak Agung (all with Istri after for a female). The brahmana (priests) have Ida Bagus for a man, Ida Ayu for a woman. Upper-class titles followed by commoner birth order names indicate intercaste marriages. So Gusti Ngurah Putu is the son of a wesia father and a jaba mother.

All of these status titles are followed by a given name.

The lakeside Pura Ulun Danu temple at Candikuning

on the neighbouring island of Lombok, you can still find the carefree attitude to life, the empty beaches and things that gave rise to the legend: exotic temples seeming to float in the waters of volcanic lakes; countryside covered with wild hydrangeas, orchids and tropical roses; village markets, ceremonies and processions not only from another world, but from another time.

Life, Architecture and Art

Everywhere in Bali, you can still stay for very little money in the guesthouses and extra rooms that thousands of Balinese families have carefully built and upgraded over the years. This can be a remarkable chance to observe Balinese life, with its intricate rituals and customs, firsthand. Bali has also developed an impressive infrastructure of hotels (in every price range), many of which are enchanting enclaves of Balinese architecture, landscape and music and dance traditions. Many

Which Beach?

Here are the main options. In addition, the Bukit Peninsula (see page 33) has some of Bali's most beautiful beaches, although the currents are strong.

Sanur: long-established beach hotels; shops and restaurants; sand beach but rocks restrict swimming at low tide. Atmosphere is somewhere between noisy Kuta and peaceful Nusa Dua. (See pages 28–29.)

Kuta: a huge sandy beach, patrolled by lifeguards; good surfing, but swim only between the red and yellow flags; the largest choice of accommodation; plenty of clothing shops; a mainly young crowd and the most active night scene in Bali. (See pages 29–31.)

Tuban Beach: the quieter continuation of Kuta beach southward; mostly larger hotels; a less hectic street scene but plenty of restaurants; family-orientated. (See page 31.)

Legian: vast beach; surfing and swimming with care; bars, discos and restaurants at southern end; the north is relatively tranquil. (See page 32.)

Seminyak: broad sandy beach north of Legian; surfing and swimming; this quiet stretch is home to several luxury hotels and a cluster of restaurants that serve some of the best food found in Bali. (See page 32.)

Nusa Dua: a resort enclave with a fine sandy beach; sailing and safe swimming; some hotels are far from outside shops and restaurants; isolated from island life and sights. (See pages 33.)

Jimbaran Beach: just a few hotels; superb gently shelving beach; sailing and safe swimming; a small village nearby; south of the airport and some way from most tourist sights. (See page 34.)

Candidasa: narrow sandy beach, rocky offshore; cottage-type accommodation in medium-low price range; handy for visiting eastern Bali and the mountains. (See page 54.)

Lovina Beach: on the north coast, furthest from the airport; a long stretch of black (actually dark grey) sand; shallow water; low- to mid-priced accommodation and a scattering of restaurants; a base for diving and visits to the mountains. (See page 65.)

hotels echo the architecture of Balinese temples or exquisite palace water gardens; others are designed to resemble thatch-roofed rustic villages. In Bali, internationally renowned architects have been allowed to create their most fabulous dreams. Wherever you choose to stay, you can immerse yourself in the Balinese experience. It is virtually mandatory for hotels to build shrines in their gardens for prayers and offerings of the staff. Some hotels actively welcome on to their grounds the many local festivals, processions, celebrations of life and death, dancers, musicians and performances that are part of the fabric of daily life in Bali.

There is no word for 'artist' in the Balinese language. Sculpture, painting, dance, music, weaving and mask-making have always been part of everyday life. Rice farmers performed the ceremonial dances they were taught as children; craftsmen created practical objects imbued with beauty and decoration; weavers created the dreamlike patterns of *ikat* cloth; houses were built with understated grace in ways that were harmonious with nature. All Balinese knew how to adorn and beautify. Today, Bali is a shopper's heaven for everything from traditional crafts to casual clothing and beachwear. Most of the crafts have been

Dance is an important part of Bali's rich cultural heritage

adapted to the tourist and export trades and are now produced in vast quantities. Ancient skills have been applied to new subjects without drastically debasing standards and something quite fresh and inventive seems to appear each year. The Balinese are truly versatile, turning to new materials, designs and techniques unknown to their parents' generation. The painted tropical fish and birds, sold in markets across the island, weren't made at all until 20 years ago; the quilted bedcovers and trendy modern homewares are newer still. A large proportion of the proceeds from this booming trade is spent by successful villagers to beautify their temples and stage ceremonies more extravagant and flamboyant than ever. The wave of tourism that has swept the island has altered Balinese culture but Bali's traditions are flourishing as never before, continuing to amaze and delight the outside world.

Surfing has become a popular activity in Bali

A BRIEF HISTORY

Today's Indonesians mainly descend from people who came from south China via the Malay peninsula and moved along the island chain to Java, Bali, Lombok and beyond, from 3000 to 1000 BC. Archaeological finds show that there was a flourishing Bronze Age culture in Bali and Lombok between about 1000 and 100 BC. Trade and cultural exchanges with Southeast Asia had certainly begun by that period, and there were frequent contacts with India by AD 100. About this time, too, wet rice cultivation was introduced to Bali, changing the face of the countryside to its present appearance of rice fields and terraces.

Indian traders and teachers brought Buddhism to Java. It also influenced Bali, where people continued in their ancient animist beliefs, worshipping the spirits of the mountains, rivers and other natural forces.

Language

Bahasa Indonesia, the official language of Indonesia, is different from Balinese, but is spoken and understood by most of Bali's 3.4 million population.

HINDUISM COMES TO BALI

In the eighth and ninth centuries AD, several Buddhist rulers in Java and their subjects converted to Hinduism and created a Shiva-Buddha cult. Eventually, people in Bali followed suit, since their local gods and spirits could be housed easily in the crowded Hindu pantheon. Around 930 AD, a queen from East Java married the king of Bali, and the conversion process accelerated. A mild form of the caste system and the concept of the Hindu trinity of Brahma, Shiva and Vishnu were introduced. But Bali was no mere vassal state of Java. From 1019 to 1042, Airlangga, son of the Balinese king Udayana, ruled over East Java, while his younger brother acted as regent in Bali. During the 12th and 13th centuries, Bali was often independent due to conflicts in Java.

A powerful Hindu empire named after its capital, Majapahit, united the whole of Java by 1320. The Majapahit general Gajah Mada reconquered Bali in 1343 and annexed a large part of the Indonesian archipelago. Hindu art and scholarship spread through the islands but on most of the islands this flowering was short-lived. With the death in 1389 of King Hayam Wuruk, the empire of Majapahit began to decline.

Pura Penataran Sasih, one of the oldest temples in Bali

Muslim traders and teachers had already started converting Java's princes and people to Islam, especially in coastal areas, and in the 14th and 15th centuries the movement spread to the interior. By 1500, seeing their world breaking up, many Majapahit aristocrats, priests and scholars moved to Bali, where their culture continued to flourish. Islam never gained a strong foothold in Bali, which was difficult to invade because of its many reefs and lack of harbours, and had few products to attract traders. The early 16th century also brought the first European ships to Indonesian waters, when the Portuguese came in search of spices and set up trading posts – though not in Bali.

In 1550, Bali was finally united in a prosperous Golden Age under Batu Renggong, the ruler of Gelgel, near Klungkung. His men even succeeded in turning back the tide of Islam for a short while, adding eastern Java and Lombok to Renggong's domains. During his rule, Balinese power, culture and influence reached a peak, with a great boom in temple building and the associated crafts of sculpture and woodcarving.

Intricate wood carvings, artistry practised for centuries

During the next 250 years, Bali's rulers fell to squabbling among themselves and the island was split into 10 or more rajadoms. Bali's contact with the Dutch was restricted to providing slaves – mainly Balinese who had broken the rajas' laws or priests' taboos – and soldiers for the army of the United Dutch East Indies Company (*Vereenigde Oostindische Compagnie*, or VOC). The company was the instrument of influence of the Netherlands until it went bankrupt in 1799 and was superseded by the government. Throughout the 18th century, Dutch influence and authority spread across Indonesia but bypassed the relatively poor, unimportant island of Bali.

Between 1811 and 1817, during the Napoleonic Wars, Britain took control of Indonesia and seriously thought of staying once the wars were over. Britain's administrator, Stamford Raffles, who was named Lieutenant Governor, even visited Bali and may have had it in mind to build a trading station here. After the war, however, the British government decided to restore Dutch territory and interests – and Raffles found another site: the island and future port of Singapore.

THE DUTCH TAKE OVER

Once re-established in Java, the Dutch attempted to increase their influence through military means. Expeditions to Bali were despatched in the 1840s, and by the end of that decade the northern and eastern parts of Bali were under Dutch rule.

For the remainder of the 19th century the Dutch, using rajas and other aristocrats as regents, took control of most of Bali but their influence in the south remained limited until 1904 when a ship wrecked off Sanur was plundered. The Dutch demanded reparations; the southern rajas refused. In 1906 a force of mainly Moluccan troops led by Dutch officers marched on Denpasar to enforce compliance. They found the place almost deserted, until suddenly the Raja of Badung, his family and courtiers emerged from the palace. On a signal

Court of the Regency of Buleleng, 1880s

from the raja, one of his priests stabbed him with a *keris* (dagger), and then, pausing only to stab their children first, the rest of the royal party began a *puputan*, either killing themselves or running suicidally towards the enemy. When the scene was repeated by the Dewa Agung and his wives and followers in 1908 in front of the palace at Klungkung, the rajas' resistance to Dutch rule was over.

The public in the Netherlands was appalled by these grisly events. From then on, Bali and the Balinese came to be looked on as unique – to be protected from the colonial treatment that had turned the other islands into plantations exploited for profit. Tourism was encouraged, and foreign visitors who did make the journey returned to the outside world with news of the island's extraordinary culture. An American couple, Bob and Louise Koke, opened the first hotel on Kuta Beach in 1936; Louise G. Koke's memoir, *Our Hotel In Bali*, provides an idyllic portrait of Bali's first, tenuous endeavour at tourism from 1936 until the Japanese invasion in 1942.

In the 1920s and 1930s Cokorda Gede Agung Sukawati, ruler of Ubud, extended a long Sukawati family tradition of patronising talent and craftsmanship by hosting visiting Western artists, including the German painter, Walter Spies, who stayed for 14 years. Spies' influence revolutionised painting in Bali, which had previously been bound by strict conventions. The Pita Maha school of young Western-influenced artists emerged (also influenced by the Dutch pastelist, Rudolf Bonnet), putting Ubud on the world map of contemporary art. Spies was deeply involved in Balinese culture, and his house and spring-fed swimming pool (now part of Ubud's Tjampuhan Hotel) – and later his house at Iseh near Sidemen – were visited by Western artists, academics, musicians and stars of theatre and film.

From 1900 until the start of World War II, many young Indonesians received a Dutch education, with the brightest students going to universities in the Netherlands. The Dutch language gave the vast polyglot archipelago a sense of unity, even among islands that had been bitter enemies for centuries. Indonesian nationalism and a movement for independence from Holland gained strength.

WAR AND INDEPENDENCE

Early in 1942, the Japanese invaded and occupied Indonesia, with the intention of exploiting its oil and rice. Until the end of World War II, the Japanese occupation continued; with the surrender of Japan in August, 1945, Indonesia declared its independence. The period from 1946 to 1949 saw the Dutch trying to reassert control; however, weakened as it was from years of Nazi occupation, the Netherlands was not able to muster the huge forces needed to recapture all the islands.

In Bali, in 1946, Indonesian nationalist fighters, led by Ngurah Rai, were trapped by Dutch forces close to Marga, north of Tabanan. Outnumbered, Ngurah Rai and all 96 of his followers were killed in what is regarded as Bali's last *puputan*. Finally on 17 August 1949, the Republic of Indonesia was recognised by the UN. Sukarno, pre-eminent in the nationalist movement, became the nation's leader. The 1955 Afro-Asian conference in Bandung heralded the arrival of the new nation. With India's Nehru and Tito of Yugoslavia, Sukarno was credited with founding the non-aligned movement.

Fallen fighters

Ngurah Rai's *puputan* near Marga is commemorated by a monument and museum at the site, together with stones bearing the names of each of those who died on Bali during the independence struggle (see page 71).

Years of Confusion

A succession of short-lived coalition governments wrestled with the problems posed by separatist movements of the various island groups, dislocation caused by war and its aftermath, a badly neglected infrastructure and the colonial legacy of over-exploited plantations. Frustrated by Indonesia's loss of direction, Sukarno declared a form of martial law in 1957. A so-called 'guided democracy' and an appointed national council and non-party government took the place of the elected assembly and ineffectual coalitions.

A young Sukarno

The period between 1959 and 1965 was a surreal time of government by means of slogans and Orwellian acronyms. Sukarno attempted to control the competing nationalist, religious and communist groups; NASAKOM was the word he used to represent their supposed common interests. Processions paraded with placards emblazoned with NAMIPOL (Sukarno's political manifesto) and DEKON (his economic declaration) written on them. In the meantime, the Indonesian economy collapsed and hyper-inflation destroyed the currency.

The country's limited foreign-exchange reserves were squandered on window-dressing projects, grand monuments, and stadiums to host the Asian Games of 1962, seen as part of a plan to bring Indonesia into the world spotlight. International travel agents were given a tour of the country, including a visit to Bali that coincided with an important Balinese ceremony in March 1963 at the so-called 'mother temple' Pura Besakih, on the slopes of the island's highest mountain, Gunung Agung. Portentously, the volcano, though long dormant, chose this particular moment to begin emitting smoke and firing rocks into the air but the ceremony went ahead anyway. The official guests had scarcely left Bali when Gunung Agung exploded in what was the most violent eruption the island had seen in centuries. Lava flowed down its slopes but despite the impressions conveyed by reporters it covered only a limited area. The chief instrument of destruction was the ash that showered down on the eastern half of Bali, covering it with a layer 40cm (15ins) thick. Crops were wiped out; the rice terraces were devastated and starvation threatened.

Ida Bagus Nyoman Rai's impression of the 1963 eruption of Gunung Agung

The ash fall also blocked rivers but the dams it formed could not retain the waters for long. When they broke, torrents of mud and rock tore down the valleys and through the villages and towns along the river banks. The official death toll of 1,600 was a wild underestimate.

Coup and Revenge

On 30 September 1965, a group of army conspirators, who claimed they acted to prevent a coup against Sukarno, kidnapped and killed six army generals and a lieutenant. In the following days, General Suharto, one of the most senior surviving commanders, isolated the conspirators and effectively seized power. The blame for the killings was pinned on the Indonesian Communist Party, the PKI, which denied involvement. A pogrom was then unleashed, first in Java and next in Bali, with widespread killings of suspected Communists.

The Chinese minority, mainly small businesspeople, were also a target. In common with the other immigrant groups, they had been compelled by law to display the flag of their country of origin, even if a century had passed since their ancestors had come to Indonesia. Throughout Indonesia, every Chinese business, marked by the flag of China, and associated in people's minds with communism, was attacked. The numbers killed will never be known: in Bali alone the total casualties may well have exceeded 100,000.

Sukarno's association with the PKI led to his being forced to yield most of his powers. Only his honoured role in the independence struggle saved him from trial. In 1968 Suharto took over the presidency.

Growth and Modernisation

In the following decades, the economy stabilised as growing oil revenues fuelled expansion. The Chinese community, the backbone of the nation's economy, rebuilt its commercial interests – although less visibly this time. Tourism became a money-spinner: the 1970s saw a rapid increase in foreign visitors. In the 1980s, the authorities decided to develop more up-market tourism in Bali, and Nusa Dua was designated a tourist enclave where only luxury hotels would be built. To bring the necessary volume of visitor traffic to fill the new rooms, Denpasar Airport's runway was extended to handle big planes. During the next decade, Bali became one of the most prosperous places in the country. In order to help Balinese better prepare for new jobs in the tourism market, English language courses became mandatory in Bali's schools.

The late 1990s were years of disillusionment, with the Suharto regime's many failings apparent and corruption widespread. As the economy faltered, ethnic conflicts erupted in many parts of the country; even Lombok experienced a brief flaring of violence against Christians and Chinese. But Bali, with its unique Hindu culture and its international, tourism-orientated outlook, remained an island of stability throughout this unsettled period of Indonesian history.

This period of calm ended suddenly on 12 October 2002, when bombs planted by Muslim terrorists exploded in Kuta, killing over 200 people and injuring many more. The economy was seriously damaged by the attacks and also by the Iraq war, but visitors had begun to return when, on 1 October 2005, terrorists struck again, in Kuta and Jimbaran, using suicide bombers. This time tourism was less affected, and the number of foreign arrivals to Bali is now higher than ever.

Bali-Hindu devotees

Historical Landmarks

3000–1000 BC Migration from southern China via Malay peninsula and along the island chain of Indonesia.

c.1000–100 BC Bronze Age culture in Bali and Lombok.

c.AD 100 Trade and cultural exchanges with Southeast Asia and India. Beginning of wet rice cultivation.

8th–9th centuries Hindu kingdoms replace Buddhist kingdoms in Java; Hinduism spreads to Bali.

10th–13th centuries Bali independent at times or ruled by Java.

1294 Majapahit empire founded in Java.

1343 Majapahit Gajah Mada reconquers Bali.

1400–1500 Rise of Islam in Java.

c.1500 Java's Hindu rulers, priests and scholars flee to Bali.

1550 Bali and Lombok ruled by Dewa Agung (god-king) of Gelgel.

1597 Dutch expedition under de Houtman arrives off Bali.

17th–18th centuries Isolation. Bali splits into ten rajadoms.

1846–1849 Dutch military expeditions.

1850–1900 The Dutch establish control over most of Bali.

1906 Dutch force marches on Denpasar. The Raja of Badung and his court commit mass suicide.

1920s–30s Foreign artists bring Balinese culture to world notice.

1927 Sukarno and others form nationalist party, PNI.

1942 Japanese occupy Indonesia, exploiting its oil and rice.

1945 World War II ends. Sukarno and Hatta proclaim republic.

1946–49 Dutch attempt to re-establish control over Indonesia.

1950 Republic of Indonesia recognized by Dutch.

1963 Eruption of Gunung Agung devastates Bali.

1980s–90s Rapid rise of tourism. Many luxury resorts are built.

2002 Terrorists bomb a Kuta nightspot on 12 October.

2003 SARS outbreak and Iraq War further affect tourism.

2005 Terrorist bombs again rock Kuta and Jimbaran.

2009 A record year for Bali tourism, with 2.2 million foreign visitors to the island.

WHERE TO GO

Bali is not a large island: you can easily reach anywhere in it in several hours. But to the Balinese, the island is their universe – a world unto itself. You will reduce travelling time and get to know different areas of Bali in depth if you make overnight stays or visits of a few days in each of the island's regions.

Don't expect to rush around seeing all the temples and other cultural attractions on the island, or all those mentioned in this section. The island scenery and fleeting glimpses of everyday life are just as rewarding. Best of all is to turn a corner and find a procession, perhaps the whole population of a village, dressed in their best and blocking the road. Balinese temples, palaces and other buildings, however exotic or exquisite, only really come to life when filled with ceremonies and the bustle of festivals. We have selected some of the most interesting and important attractions but to truly appreciate and absorb what you see, we suggest you take a few at a time.

THE SOUTHERN RESORTS

Most of Bali's tourism is concentrated in a tiny fraction of the island, with the vast majority of visitors heading for the beach areas of **Sanur**, **Kuta**, **Seminyak** and **Nusa Dua**, all within a short drive of the airport. Some stretches of sand are so magnificent and the water so warm that it's hard to believe that they were ignored for so long by the Balinese people, who have traditionally turned away from the sea. Now visitors come in the millions from all over the world with little in mind but sun, sand, warm seas and watersports.

Pura Tanah Lot, one of Bali's most important sea temples

Visitors flock to Sanur for the warm waters and fine sands

Sanur

Southeast of Denpasar, Bali's capital, is **Sanur**. In atmosphere, Sanur falls somewhere between noisy Kuta and secluded Nusa Dua. Half-hidden by tropical gardens and foliage, many of Sanur's hotels are small in scale and face the pleasant, sandy beach. The water is generally calm, protected from waves and undercurrents by an outlying coral reef. At high tide, the swimming is wonderful, but at low tide, the water dips to knee or waist level, and wading is the only activity possible.

Just inland, parallel to the beach, Sanur looks at first like nothing more than a long strip of souvenir shops, clothing boutiques and restaurants. But take a walk along some of the lanes leading off the main road, Jalan Tanjung Sari, or beyond the impatient traffic of the bypass (Jalan Bypass) and you'll find traditional life still going on as if tourism had never happened. Many small Indonesian and seafood restaurants on the street are pleasant; one or two are outstanding.

Only a short walk north along the shore from the 10-storey Inna Grand Bali Beach Hotel is the **Le Mayeur Museum** (Tue–Sun 8am–2pm; charge), once the house of the Belgian painter, Adrien Jean Le Mayeur. He came to Bali in 1932 and stayed to marry the beautiful Ni Polok, who had been a well-known *legong* dancer *(see page 91)* before retiring (at 14!) to teach dance. In its day, the garden with its ponds and statues was open on the seaward side; now it is enclosed. The outside of the house is covered with stone carvings, while the interior is a gallery of sculpture collected by Le Mayeur. The walls are hung with his own paintings: European landscapes, Balinese scenes and studies of dancers, mostly Ni Polok. When Le Mayeur died in 1958, the house was turned into a museum.

Low-rise haven

Sanur is where the first modern tourist hotel, 10 storeys high, was built in the 1960s. Fortunately, no other high-rise hotels have been built in Bali since then – the authorities decreed that in the future no building should be higher than the tallest coconut palm (15m/50ft).

Near the small harbour at this end of Sanur Beach you can find motorised *prahu* (outrigger boats) to take you to **Nusa Lembongan**, an island 17km (11 miles) offshore to the east, which is noted for its good surfing and snorkelling.

At the southern end of Sanur Beach, near the Sanur Beach Hotel, the signs point to **Pura Belanjong**. It's only a short walk, but few people find their way to this old temple, which is deserted unless there's a ceremony.

Kuta

The most famous stretch of beach in Bali forms the western shore of a narrow neck of land just north of the airport. After travellers in the 1960s discovered that they could enjoy a back-to-nature existence here at minimal cost, they gathered in increasing numbers. Tales were told in Australia about the 'perfect wave', and Kuta became every surfer's dream destination. Once a poor fishing village and wasteland believed to be inhabited by bad spirits, by the 1980s it was transformed into a frenetic scene, fuelled by alcohol and, for a while, illegal drugs. A shantytown soon sprang up. Theft and prostitution – as well as unregulated street hawkers – seemed to be becoming endemic. Today, the drugs have largely disappeared but you should beware of pickpockets and shouldn't leave property unguarded. Traffic is a nightmare.

Kuta, and its progressively upscale neighbours to the north – Legian, Seminyak and Kerobokan (as well as Tuban, to the south) – provide an enormous selection of hotels, restaurants and shops. You'll find some of the best Italian, French, vegetarian, Greek, Spanish, Moroccan, Japanese, Korean, Indian and Indonesian restaurants on the island, as well as some of the best shops for crafts from other islands, fashion, locally produced *ikat* cloth, and casual Bali-style beach clothing.

The beach is the real reason to be here, and even though you won't escape the hawkers, it's a rest cure after the bustle of the town. Swim only between the flags, where lifeguards keep watch: the undertow and currents can be hazardous.

Old Hands

Kuta's beach masseuses are an institution: Some have been operating here for 20 years. In the heat of the day they understandably prefer to work in the shade of an awning. Negotiate a price first and check that there's no sand on you, on the cloth where you'll be lying or on the masseuse's hands, otherwise you'll feel as if you've been rubbed with sandpaper. Massage has a central and respected role in Balinese healing, and although the beach version is rudimentary, most of the more upmarket hotels and spas employ highly skilled practitioners.

A stroll along the beach

At sunset, a golden light reflects off the sea and local people come out to stroll or paddle in the shallows. Young men play soccer on the sand or join the tourists in a volleyball game, while the eager beach masseuses rustle up a new wave of business. Come nightfall, new choices beckon. You can inspect Bali's selection of shops, pick a restaurant, go on a pub crawl, or wait for midnight when the clubs get into gear.

Tuban, Legian and Seminyak

Kuta Beach can mean the small area around the original village, or the whole coast stretching from the airport north to Legian and beyond. Kuta's neighbours are developing separate identities. **Tuban Beach** to the south has many big hotels, a huge shopping mall and a waterpark with waterslides and a swimming pool, attracting families and groups. The beach has calmer water and streets are quieter; however, sea pollution can sometimes be a problem here.

Adjoining Kuta to the north, **Legian** at first seems like more of the same, with a big concentration of places to eat, drink, dance and sleep along Jalan Melasti, Jalan Yudisthira and Jalan Raya Legian itself. Sunrise is an idyllic time to be on Legian Beach. Surfers are out at the first light of dawn and runners pace the water's edge.

4 A little further north is hip-and-vibrant **Seminyak**, which boasts the trendiest boutiques and homeware stores on the island, along with the highest concentration of independent fine-dining restaurants, and a wide choice of bars, nightclubs, spas, stylish hotels and sumptuous holiday rental villas. The atmosphere is much more sophisticated than Kuta and the beach is quieter during the day. The pulsating nightlife and luxurious accommodation draw a fashionable crowd of people, especially Europeans. Nowhere, in recent years, has the upmarket development of Bali been more evident than here.

Floral offerings

Check out **Jalan Laksmana** and **Jalan Abimanyu** (also known as Dhyana Pura). The former street is home to dozens of restaurants, which serve all kinds of cuisines, while along the latter you will find a string of live music bars, gay bars and clubs. There are also some chic home furnishing and decor stores along **Jalan Raya Seminyak**.

North again, surfers find their way to **Canggu Beach** by way of narrow roads through the rice fields. This is now a developing area with many luxury villas.

Bukit Badung and Nusa Dua

Referred to simply as Bukit (or 'the hill') by the Balinese, the peninsula south of the airport is almost a separate island. Most of it is a windswept limestone plateau, entirely unlike the rest of southern Bali. Too dry for rice, its rocky soil is used to grow beans, cassava and peanuts. The dramatic coastline is pounded by Bali's most challenging surf and, in the early 1970s, those in search of the perfect wave discovered some thrilling breaks, hidden coves and golden-sand beaches. At the time there was almost no infrastructure. Now the most exclusive destination on the island, the Bukit presents some of Bali's most glamorous villas and boutique hotels as well as the New Kuta Golf Course at Pecatu.

On the eastern side of the peninsula is **Nusa Dua**, a tourist ◀ **5** enclave of wide paved lanes and manicured gardens, and the 'Bali Collection' – a shopping mall and restaurant complex – to support the many five-star resorts. Here, the outside world – including even the everyday Balinese world – is excluded. As at Sanur, when the tide is out, the water is too low for swimming, but most Nusa Dua hotels have vast swimming pools. There's little traffic or noise and no hassle from hawkers in this ribbon-wrapped hotel zone.

Jutting into the bay, north of Nusa Dua, lies **Tanjung** ◀ **6** **Benoa**, a slender, 5-km (3-mile) long peninsula, which points like a finger towards Benoa Harbour. On the tip, the village of **Benoa** was once a bustling trading port, but today the area is a watersports arena of jet skis, motorboats, diving centres, bars and hotels, including the prestigious Conrad Resort.

Don't confuse Tanjung Benoa (Benoa village) with **Benoa Port**, which is located on the opposite (north) side of the muddy inlet known as Benoa Harbour. Reached from the Sanur-Kuta road by a long causeway, the harbour is used by cargo ships, day cruisers, cruise ships, flying boats and the fast boat ferry services. There is a charge if you wish to drive along the causeway to the jetty, but there is no reason for going to the end unless you plan to take a cruise to Nusa Lembongan or a deep-sea fishing trip.

Jimbaran Beach

7 ▶ **Jimbaran Beach** is a great arc of sand facing a sheltered bay south of the airport, shared by an increasing number of resorts and hotels, and what was once a sleepy fishing village. The golden-sand beach, however, remains relaxed and peaceful, and due to an offshore coral reef, the sea is generally safe for swimming. What makes Jimbaran really famous is its fresh fish, traded daily at the nearby Kedonganan fish market. At sunset, the west-facing beach becomes a major attraction when bus loads of visitors come to partake in the seafood feasts served up in the many beachfront cafés.

Fish catch at Jimbaran Beach

The road across the Bukit peninsula climbs past limestone quarries to a height of 200m (660ft) on its way to the western tip of land and

Monkey business at Pura Luhur Uluwatu

Pura Luhur Uluwatu, an 11th-century Hindu temple balanced on the very edge of the perpendicular cliffs, some 70m (230ft) above the ocean. The area around the temple is inhabited by a band of mischievous monkeys, who snatch tourists' unguarded items, so don't wear a hat, sunglasses, dangling earrings or anything else that can be yanked away from you. A Kecak Balinese Dance performance takes place daily here at 6pm.

DENPASAR AND UBUD

The capital of Bali since the end of World War II, **Denpasar** has been fuelled by prosperity from the tourism boom. With all the government institutions and buildings to match its status, it's a noisy, polluted urban sprawl. Rush hour lasts most of the day and when traffic lights change there's a cavalry charge of motorcycles and cars. In the middle of it all, the better-off live in traditional family compounds – extra-high walls are the main concession to this kind of life. Those who have had to adapt to apartment living in the city can still have their family temple – on the roof!

The most prominent central landmark is a big grey statue of the four-faced Hindu god, Catur Muka, looking each way at the main intersection. The one-way system here sends traffic north up **Jalan Veteran** or east along **Jalan Surapati** which, after changes of name, becomes the road to Sanur. West of the intersection, **Jalan Gajah Mada** is lined with banks, shops and restaurants. It soon meets Jalan Sulawesi and then the dirty and often rather smelly Badung River. The city's main fresh produce market, **Pasar Badung**, jams a four-storey building and is open from before dawn until midday. Just across the river is a similar building housing the craft and textile market, **Pasar Kumbasari**.

Transport options in downtown Denpasar

The colonial **Inna Bali Hotel** stands on both sides of Jalan Veteran. A little further along on the left there's another market. Approximately 1km (½ mile) along Jalan Veteran, the **bird market** caters to the local liking for caged birds, which range from large hornbills to tiny songsters; other animals are also sold here.

The big area of grass south of Jalan Surapati is **Taman Puputan** (Puputan Square), site of the *puputan* or mass suicide in 1906 of the Raja of Badung's court *(see page 19)*.

At the furthest corner of Puputan Square, you'll find the **Bali Museum** (Museum Negeri Propinsi Bali; Sat–Thur 8am–4pm, Fri 8.30–1pm; charge). This interesting but rather antiquated museum of ethnography, history and art was created by the Dutch in 1937. Three of the four museum buildings represent different styles of Balinese palace architecture. The main building contains historical artefacts, ranging from a 2,200-year-old stone sarcophagus to photographs of the 1906 *puputan;* upstairs is a collection of day-to-day and household items. The First Pavilion, designed in the Singaraja style, displays antique Balinese textiles; the Second Pavilion, in the 18th-century Karangasaem style, houses religious and ceremonial objects; the Third Pavilion, designed in the style of the Tabanan Regency, displays artefacts used in music and dance, including a collection of masks, puppets and costumes. The museum is not strong on catalogues or explanatory labels; your best bet is to enjoy the displays for their own intrinsic beauty.

The temple adjoining the museum compound is the recently constructed **Pura Jagatnata**, built mainly out of white coral and dedicated to Sanghyang Widi, the Supreme God. Of the many Hindu gods, the trinity of Brahma, Vishnu and Shiva is considered to be pre-eminent, but a single god of whom all others are manifestations ties in conveniently with the Indonesian *pancasila,* or national code.

The tiny Catholic community attends **St Joseph's Church** on Jalan Kepundung, off Jalan Surapati, a building thatched with palm fronds and with six distinctly Balinese-looking angels carved in stone standing above the door.

The imposing **Arts Centre** (Taman Werdi Budaya; Tue–Sun 8am–5pm; charge), off Jalan Nusa Indah, has a permanent exhibition of paintings and woodcarvings and an arena for dance and drama. The major **Bali Arts Festival** is held here every June and July. Ask about chances to see dancers and musicians practising, as well as regular performances for visitors. You can also see dance nearby at the **Sekolah Tinggi Seni Indonesia**, formerly the Indonesian Academy of Dance and still a dance academy.

Renon, in the southeast, is where most government buildings are gathered, including the main post office, many consulates and the tourist information office.

From Denpasar to Ubud: The Craft Villages

When the rajas ruled Bali, they organised the various crafts on a village basis. One village would specialise in wood-carving, another in weaving, and a third in basketry. Passed down through each family, today those same skills are still practised in the same communities. Along the busy road north from Denpasar to Ubud, the various craft villages have virtually merged into each other, but you can tell which one you're in by their products.

The village of **Batubulan** (moonstone) specialises in carving statues, friezes and ornaments out of soft grey *paras* stone. Easily shaped, it just as easily wears away, so outdoor temple decorations last only a few decades, and there is a constant demand for replacements. Bug-eyed demons and tranquil heads of the Buddha, each different, line the road and fill the yards of the many workshops. Batubulan's temple is naturally a showcase. The *barong* dance *(see page 92)*, staged every

Finished carvings at Batubulan

morning here, is a totally commercial production attended by busloads of tourists. At the **Taman Barung Bali Bird Park** (daily 9am–5.30pm; charge), which is located just north of Batubulan, you will find more than 1,000 specimens representing 250 species of exotic birds in well-designed, walk-through aviaries. Next door at the reptile park you can see the famous Indonesian Komodo dragon lizards.

Celuk (pronounced *Cheluk*), between Ubud and Denpasar, is a centre for hundreds of silversmiths and goldsmiths, their shops and workplaces line the main road and spill down every *gang*. Using only simple hand tools, these craftsmen can produce any style of jewellery, from ornate pieces with semi-precious stones to delicate filigree work or modern designs. Tour buses make a regular stop at one of the big galleries, but prices should be lower down the small lanes.

Stop in nearby **Sukawati** for wind-chimes, puppets, basketry, ceremonial umbrellas, quilts and jewellery. Many stalls have

Barong mask from Batuan

been brought together in the big **Pasar Seni** building.

Like Ubud, **Batuan** developed a distinctive painting style in the 1930s when Western techniques influenced the local artists *(see page 51)*. Dark forest green and black predominate in the early Batuan pictures, relieved by flashes of white and amber. The village is still a centre for art: Painters today feature surfers and photographers, as well as Jeep-loads of tourists among the massed figures in their pictures. The main temple, Pura Desa Batuan, is especially lavish in its carving decoration. A short diversion eastwards will bring you to **Blahbatuh**, where the palace compound, Puri Blahbatuh, is now a commercial orchid nursery, sometimes referred to as Puri Anggrek (Orchid Palace).

Nearby, **Belega** specialises in bamboo, producing massive pieces of furniture. You'll see them on display along the main street and in some of Bali's hotels. Then comes **Bona**, a centre of basketry, which also bills itself as the home of the *kecak* dance. The regular performances here are certainly more complete than most versions.

❿ Back on the road to Ubud: **Mas** is famous for its woodcarvers, furniture makers and mask-carvers. Vast numbers of shops and workshops line the long main street. Unless a shop has been specifically recommended, just stop anywhere and look inside, without buying right away. Then investigate the side streets. Away from the traffic, you might find an entire family producing wooden hangings for the export market.

Ubud

Once a magnet for foreign artists and still home to some, **Ubud** and the cluster of villages around it form the cultural and artistic focus of Bali. An increasing number of visitors come on day trips from the coastal resorts but a better plan is to stay overnight or longer. There's a wide choice of accommodation, ranging from cheap homestays and charming middle-range hotels to high-priced luxury hideaways on the river gorges just outside Ubud.

The day trippers only have enough time to see the commercialism and chaos in Ubud's main streets. Just a short walk away, however, are the green, peaceful rice terraces and jungle-filled river gorges that have captivated Bali's visitors for decades and are so much a part of the region's mystique.

To find out the schedules of dance performances and other events in the vicinity, pay an early visit to the Bina Wisata

Legong dance performance in Ubud

Pasar Bali by Anak Agung Gde Sobrat at the Puri Lukisan

information office on Jalan Raya, the main thoroughfare. Excellent, very inexpensive performances of traditional dance are offered in the atmospheric compound beside the palace in the centre of town. In addition to its many shops, markets and galleries, Ubud is home to a number of interesting museums.

Museum Puri Lukisan (daily 9am–4pm; charge) on Jalan Raya Ubud is one of Ubud's most attractive museums. In lush gardens, a fine hall has been built to house the works from the collection of the Dutch painter, Rudolf Bonnet, and that of his patron, Cokorda Gede Agung Sukawati, who governed Ubud for many decades. Look for the work of I Gusti Nyoman Lempad, one of the first artists to adopt Western techniques and bring the flat *wayang* figures of traditional painting to life. Remarkably, he was probably over 50 years old when he met Walter Spies and Bonnet *(see page 51)*. Even he did not know his exact age; it is estimated that when he died, in 1978, he was 116. I Gusti Nyoman Lempad was chief architect and sculptor to the ruling Sukawati family of Ubud and designed the beautiful **Pura Taman Kumuda Saraswati** temple on Jalan Raya.

The superb **Neka Art Museum** (daily 9am–5pm; charge), located 2km (1½ miles) out of town to the north of Campuhan, was founded in 1976 by a local dealer and collector, Suteja Neka. The views from the museum are spectacular. In five galleries you can see the work of the

Europeans who were so influential, as well as that of the finest local artists. Every piece is fully documented with informative labels; and the multilingual staff are very friendly and knowledgeable.

Some of the most striking pictures are by Indonesians working in a purely Western idiom. While others were creating new Balinese styles, they wholeheartedly adopted Western ways: Only in their subject matter do these so-called 'Academic painters' reveal their origins. A photo gallery features prints of dance and everyday life in Bali in the 1930s. The museum has a large bookstore, attractive gift shop and breezy snack shop.

The **Senawati Gallery of Art By Women** (Tue–Sun 9am–5pm), on Jalan Sriwedari, off Jalan Rayal in Ubud, houses a very worthwhile collection of paintings by local and expatriate women artists.

Other museums and galleries to visit include those of the late Antonio Blanco, a Philippine-born Spanish artist noted for erotic subject matter, and the late Han Snel, a Dutch

Sacred Geometry

Balinese temples are surrounded by walls – in fact, pura, the word for temple, means a walled area. Each temple is orientated on a mountain–sea or east–west axis. One usually enters the sacred compound from the kelod (the direction of the sea) or west side. Kaja (the direction of the mountains) and kangin (the east) are where the most holy shrines are placed. The sunrise side of the temple is holier than the sunset side, and is usually filled with secondary shrines.

The exotic, pagoda-like meru, with its multi-tiered roofs, is a dwelling place or passageway for a deity or an ancestral spirit. The meru is only built with an odd number of tiers; eleven is the maximum and indicates the highest diety.

Kites for sale on Ubud market

artist whose highly praised work is displayed in a gallery adjacent to his guesthouse, Siti Bungalows.

Near Ubud: West and North

At the western end of town, an old suspension bridge and a new road bridge cross the Campuhan river. On the north side is the temple of **Pura Gunung Labah**, which may date from the 8th century AD, making it one of Bali's earliest. Shrouded in dense vegetation, the temple overlooks Goa Raksasa, a cave named after the evil giant who is said to have lived there.

Just north of the Campuhan bridges, the Tjampuhan Hotel (sporting the old spelling) stands where Walter Spies *(see page 51)* came to live in the 1930s. Across the road and up the hill, stone stairs lead to rice fields and the track to the home of the Young Artists group at **Penestanan**. At neighbouring **Sayan**, Westerners have built their homes overlooking the rice terraces and the spectacular Ayung gorge.

The road from Campuhan past the Museum Neka leads to **Kedewatan** town, where the most luxurious hotels in the area offer similarly stunning views into the Ayung valley. Beyond Payangan, the little-used road wends its way through scenic countryside all the way to Batur *(see page 60)*.

Try to be in **Petulu**, 6km (4 miles) north of Ubud, by about 5pm. Every evening at sunset, thousands of white herons return from a day's fishing in the rice fields and glide in to roost in the trees.

> ### Beware macaques
>
> The macaques of Sacred Monkey Forest can be very mischievous, but are fascinating to watch. Vendors will sell you bananas if you want to feed them, but remember to stay on the paved pathways and don't provoke them – a bite can be dangerous.

Southern Side of Ubud

Off the main street near the information office, Monkey Forest Road heads south, against the flow of traffic, past lines of homestays, hotels, shops, galleries and restaurants. After almost 2km (just over 1 mile) it reaches the **Sacred Monkey Forest** (daily 8am–6pm; charge), an ecological reserve, home to about 300 long-tailed grey Balinese macaques. There are three ancient temples here, including the bathing temple down a flight of ornately carved stone steps next to a river.

Peliatan is known for its dances and gamelan music as well as painting and carving – 'parasite carvings' *(see page 95)* are a recent speciality. The Agung Rai Gallery sells some of the best and most expensive modern Balinese paintings.

At **Pengosekan**, just a short walk further south and west, the painters concentrate on images of birds in idyllic 'Garden of Eden' landscapes. The **Agung Rai Museum of Art** (ARMA; daily 9am–6pm; charge) displays Indonesian and European paintings.

Rice cultivation at Tegalalang

EAST OF UBUD

Two of Bali's most impressive archaeological finds are concentrated in two small areas: one close to Ubud, another 13km (8 miles) away to the northeast, near Tampaksiring.

Goa Gajah

13 Closest to Ubud in **Bedulu** village is the **Elephant Cave** or **Goa Gajah**, probably dating from the 10th century AD, cut into the hillside below the road just east of Teges. When the cave mouth was rediscovered in 1923, the huge face carved around it was mistaken for an elephant's head and the name has stuck. Inside the mouth, a passage measuring 12m (39ft) long leads to a plain transverse chamber 3.5m (11ft) wide, 20m (66ft) long and high enough to stand up in. Dim electric lights reveal niches at either end that are believed to have housed shrines: one now holds a damaged statue of the elephant-headed god, Ganesha; the other is home to a triple *lingga* (phallic images) carved from a single block of stone.

Later excavations revealed an 11th-century bathing pool on the terrace in front of the cave, with fountains in the shape of two male and four female deities. Steep stairs behind the pool leads to ruined reliefs and a niche with an ancient statue of a headless Buddha.

Yeh Pulu

Less than 1km (about ½ mile) east of Goa Gajah, look for a signpost to **Yeh Pulu** pointing to the right, down a quiet village street. The road soon ends but a footpath continues through rice terraces and past the local bathing pool. The rock face on the left of the path is carved in a series of scenes about 25m (82ft) long. Quite different from the usual Balinese style, the simple, bold and naturalistic figures include a prince and his servants out hunting wild boar with a woman clinging to his horse. The carvings probably date from the 14th century but, like Goa Gajah, the site was excavated only in the 1920s.

Pejeng

North of Yeh Pulu and the village of Bedulu, the archaeological **Museum Purbakala Gedong Arca** (Tue–Sun 8.30am–2pm; charge) brings together the neolithic and Bronze Age relics unearthed in this area, including stone sarcophagi dating from about 500 BC.

Several temples in the area are worth a short stop. **Pura Kebo Edan** has a statue of a giant deity, which measures 3m (10ft) tall, has a pierced penis and is trampling on a demon. A collection of ancient statuary includes examples from the 13th century. There's more fine carved stonework at the 14th-century **Pura Pusering Jagat**, the 'Temple of the Navel of the World'. At full moon, childless couples pray at the stone shrines depicting *lingga* and *yoni* (male and female genitalia).

At **Pura Penataran Sasih**, a great hollow bronze drum cast in one piece and measuring 1.5m (5ft) across, stands high up on a platform at the back of the temple. The style is typical of the Dong-son Bronze Age dynasty of Vietnam dating from about 300 BC, but whether it was brought to Bali or made here is unknown – according to legend, it fell from the sky. A section of the drum was broken out of it at some time in the past and only the geometric patterns are visible from ground level; decoration not in view includes faces with staring eyes.

A wooden sculpture of Rama and Sita being tempted by a deer.

Tampaksiring

To the north of **Pejeng** region the road climbs for 10km (6 miles) to **Tampaksiring**, where craft shops compete to entice tour buses to stop on their way to Batur (*see page 60*). In the middle of the long village street, look for a sign pointing down a road to the right towards **Gunung Kawi**, 1.5km (1 mile) away. A long flight of steps descends into a valley lined by stalls selling bright sarongs, carved coconut shells and cold drinks. The drink vendors can well afford to be patient – the hot, thirsty and tired tourists toiling back up the hill are a captive market.

At the bottom of the steps,

a narrow passage and gateway cut through solid rock opens out suddenly into the temple area. To the left, two rows of hollows have been carved out of the cliffs on either side of a ravine. Legend says they're the marks of a giant's fingernails, scraped out in a single night. (The head of the giant, Kebo Iwa, is carved out in stone at **Pura Gaduh**, in Blahbatuh; *see page 40*.) The rock was sculpted so as to leave a *candi* (shrine) measuring 7m

Bathing at Pura Tirtha Empul

(23ft) in each hollow, believed to be some 11th-century memorials to a royal dynasty.

Not to be confused with the place Gunung Kawi, the temple of **Pura Gunung Kawi Sebatu** is some way away in the village of Sebatu, and often many visitors asking for directions have been sent there by mistake. In fact, it is worth the trip, partly for the sights and scenery en route. From Tampaksiring the road opposite the turning to Tirta Empul twists through **Tegalalang**, a village that specialises in the mass production of woodcarvings. You'll see rows of identical ducks alongside armies of chess pieces and perhaps some original new design of statue that hasn't yet hit the shops. Two successive right turns, signposted, lead to Sebatu and Pura Gunung Kawi Sebatu, a brightly painted temple with sacred springs feeding water to ponds and bathing pools.

At the northern edge of Tampaksiring, the road forks right. Immediately on the left is the temple and holy spring of **Pura Tirtha Empul**, source of the river that flows through

Gunung Kawi. It is believed to have been created by the god Indra to revive his ailing army, who had been poisoned by an enemy. He pierced the earth, and out flowed *tirtha,* the water of immortality. It is still thought by many to have healing powers, and the pools here are often thronged with those seeking purification.

The temple is situated against a wooded hillside, in contrast to the nearby souvenir shops, which are some of the less attractive in Bali. High above the temple stands a government rest house built by the Dutch and turned into a palace by the late President Sukarno, who, they say, kept a telescope trained on the women's pool.

Women weaving double *ikat* fabric in Gianyar

EASTERN BALI

In contrast to the softer south, the mountain slopes here reach down to the sea, creating rocky shores and small bays. Where there is sand, it's grey or white streaked with silver, the result of the weathering of old lava. The rajas once ruled most of Bali from their capitals at Karangasem (now Amlapura) and Klungkung. Approaching from the south, the road passes through busy **Gianyar**, also a former raja's capital. The brick palace in the centre of town is still the home of his family and is not open to the public. Weaving is the main industry, and a number of small factories and some work-shops along the road from Ubud are open for tours. Here you can learn about making *ikat* (*endek* in Balinese), using threads that have been tie-dyed in bunches before weaving.

Klungkung

The dynasty founded by Batu Renggong was paramount in Bali for some 300 years, first ruling from Gelgel and then moving to **Klungkung** in 1710. Standing high above the mod-ern town where its broad main streets cross is the compound of an old palace (daily 9am–5pm; charge), which comprises a few main structures. The **Bale Kerta Gosa** (Royal Hall of Justice) was built at the time of the move and continued as a courthouse under the Dutch. The ceiling is covered in vivid paintings in a style unique to the region. Although the paint-ings have frequently been restored and in fact entirely replaced more than once, the work has always been done by artists

Balinese Painting

When the royal court moved from Gelgel to Klungkung in the 17th cen-tury, painters from the nearby village of Kamasan decorated the new pavilions with scenes using mainly red, ochre, white, black and brown natural pigments.

The example of Western artists who came to live in Bali led local painters to try something new. Two who settled in Ubud in the 1930s, Walter Spies and Rudolf Bonnet, were the most influential, teaching per-spective, shading, correct anatomy – everything that was lacking in the Kamasan tradition. Ubud's artists began to produce busy scenes of every-day life with naturalistic figures set against dense vegetation. When the world thinks of Balinese paintings, this is the style that comes to mind, reminding some people of the work of Rousseau.

from the nearby village of Kamasan, and it is likely that the designs resemble the 18th-century originals. Many of the panels relate tales from Balinese mythology but visitors' eyes tend to be drawn to the series depicting the dreadful punishments awaiting evildoers in the Underworld.

Important guests were received in the exquisite **Bale Kambang**, a pavilion with a painted ceiling that illustrates more lyrical stories from Balinese legends. Facing the palace garden, the **Semarajaya Museum** has been opened in one of the old buildings. Some of the most impressive exhibits are the photographs of the rajas and their families, dating from before 1908, the year of the *puputan* which took place in the open space in front of the palace and marked the end of effective resistance to the Dutch *(see page 19)*. Across the street, the **Puputan Klungkung Monument**, erected in 1992, commemorates that tragic event.

The painted ceiling of the Bale Kambang pavilion, Klungkung

West of Klungkung, a lane leads to **Tihingan**, one of four places in Bali where the gongs for gamelan orchestras are made. Another is Sawan, near the north coast *(see page 67).* In any of the bronze foundries making gongs for gamelan orchestras, the bellows keep a charcoal fire blazing, while the smiths hammer away. The place is in semi-darkness so that workers can judge the temperature of the glowing metal by its colour. The noise can be deafening and the heat unbearable, but it's well worth going to see a process that has remained virtually unchanged for centuries.

On the eastern periphery of Klungkung a bridge crosses the gorge of the Unda river, which is used as a big communal bath every afternoon as the sun goes down. Ash, mud and stones from the 1963 eruption of the Gunung Agung devastated this region, and it took many years for agriculture to recover.

Goa Lawah

Goa Lawah (Bat Cave) and its temple are hemmed in by souvenir stalls, aggressive hawkers, sash dispensers, donation collectors, ticket sellers and parked tour buses. Once past this obstacle course, you'll see the cave mouth and a seething mass of leathery bats clinging to the rock face, here and there dropping off, circling and then coming in to land again. They can't all find a place in the cave, so some hang outside in broad daylight.

On the foreshore near Goa Lawah, a few people harvest salt. Seawater is concentrated by solar evaporation and then transferred to hollowed-out palm tree trunks to crystallise.

Visiting the bat cave

If you are staying anywhere near Goa Lawah, perhaps at Candidasa, you might time a visit here for dusk. That's when the bat colony pours out of the cave like a liquid black stream and wheels away into the distance to feed on the myriad insects of the tropical night.

Umbrellas at a local temple festival, Padangbai

Padangbai

This little port stands on Bali's only natural harbor that has an unobstructed approach from the sea. The first Dutch ships dropped anchor in the sheltered bay in 1597 *(see page 14)*. Today's cruise ships usually do the same, and their passengers are ferried ashore for sightseeing excursions.

A regular passenger and car ferry makes several sailings per day to Lombok. The voyage can be rough and may take longer than the scheduled four hours. Many visitors opt to fly or take the fast boat services to Lombok from Bali, but backpackers and most locals prefer this traditional, albeit less comfortable, route. Fishermen land their catches at Padangbai's small busy beach, which is jammed with boats, just to the north of the main jetty. Facing it at the far end are two or three simple but adequate cottage-style homestays. You can arrange diving or fishing trips here but the water in the bay looks too dirty for swimming.

Beyond Padangbai comes the broad sweep of Amuk Bay, site of an oil terminal. At its eastern end, after the coast road crosses an iron bridge, a track leads down to the sea at the village of Buitan, also called **Balina Beach**, the name of its main hotel and scuba-diving centre.

Candidasa (pronounced *Chandi Dasa*)

Cottage-style hotels and homestays began to be built along this stretch of coast in the late 1970s. People looking for somewhere quieter than Kuta and lower prices than at Sanur and Nusa Dua liked the easy-going atmosphere, the sandy beach and snorkelling over the reef. However, in the 1980s, the coral reef was mined and destroyed for cement to build new hotels, the beach it had protected was washed away and the shoreline quickly eroded. In an attempt to stem the loss, ugly jetties were built and a network of concrete blocks was planted into the sea. The erosion has been stopped, but probably not reversed. There's still some sand exposed during low tide, mixed with broken coral, so it is advisable to wear shoes if you want to swim in the sea. If nothing else, the beach erosion has helped to keep Candidasa a quiet place, well stocked with hotel rooms and restaurants; it has also halted plans that would have led to even more development.

In an island of varied villages, **Tenganan** is one of the strangest. From Candidasa, it is 4km (2½ miles) inland. The residents there are Bali Aga ('original Balinese') and many of their customs and rituals date from the days before the advent of Hinduism. They have their own music and dances. Marriage outside the community used to be forbidden and the population shrank. Once the rule was eased, the downsizing trend halted.

The road from the coast terminates at a parking area outside the village walls,

Carrying offerings to the temple in Tenganan

Stepping stones at Taman Tirtagangga water garden

where you are asked to make a donation before entering. One long street climbs up from the main gateway, past a succession of open-sided pavilions and up cobblestoned terraces. By day it becomes a continuous market, with some unusually chatty, cheerful shopkeepers.

The weavers of Tenganan are well known for making *geringsing* cloth, a double *ikat (see page 96)*, in which both warp and weft threads are tie-dyed in bunches before weaving. The intricacy of the process of lining up the patterns can only be imagined: it takes months to make a single sarong, and prices are high. You'll see a lot of cloth that is printed or single *ikat*.

Amlapura (Karangasem)

North of Candidasa the road turns inland, crossing hills and fertile valleys, with views of the volcanic cone of Gunung Agung. The volcano's eruption led to a change to the town's

19 name. **Amlapura** was known as Karangasem before 1963. That is still the name of the regency, but its capital wanted to erase the memory of Mount Agung's eruption and perhaps confuse evil spirits that might still want to destroy the town of Karangasem. Part of the raja's palace and gardens were damaged then but there has been some restoration and one of three palaces at the site, **Puri Agung Karangasem**, is open to visitors.

The last raja built two elaborate water gardens. **Taman Sukasada Ujung** (daily 8am–6pm; charge) on the coast was built in the 1920s. It was destroyed by an earthquake in 1976 and underwent a long-drawn restoration. In 2004, it finally reopened and is once more worthy of a visit, even though it still looks a little stark.

From Ujung, a coast road skirts the eastern tip of Bali, but it is potholed and crosses many river beds, usually dry but impassable after heavy rain. The scenery is not varied enough to make the bumpy two-hour ride to Amed worth the effort. There's a much more beautiful alternative: taking in the raja's second fancy creation, the water playground in the hills, **Taman Tirtagangga** (daily 8am–6pm; charge), 5km (3 miles) northwest of Amlapura. This water garden was established after World War II and it was spared serious damage in the Gunung Agung eruption in 1963. You can cool off in the spring-fed pools built for the raja's family and there are places to stay if you want to enjoy the refreshing air and magical dawn light.

On the road north, a right fork at Culik leads eastwards to a series of quiet fishing and salt-panning villages, collectively known as **Amed**, spread out along several kilometres **20** of gravelly beaches. Here, many *losmen* (small, family-run hotels), as well as a few pleasant middle-range hotels, have sprung up to serve travellers who come to snorkel and dive in the clear waters.

Gunung Agung, the volacano that erupted over Bali in 1963

THE MOUNTAINS

To the Balinese, the mountains are the abode of the gods, the source of the rivers that water their crops and of occasional outbursts of destructive fury. The highest of them are volcanoes: Gunung Batur simmers more or less continuously, while Gunung Agung erupts violently once every few hundred years. When you set out for the higher altitudes, be prepared for cold with damp mists, or for scorching sunshine. Either is possible. Tour companies run day trips, sometimes combining visits to Besakih *(see page 62)* and Penelokan *(see page 59)*. This is an easy way to see the views but you will arrive at the same time as hundreds of others. Think about overnighting at a mountain resort or an inexpensive guest house. If you plan to climb one of the peaks – not a mountaineering feat but a few hours' or a full day's hill walking and scrambling over rocks – it's essential to stay nearby and start early.

Bangli

On the main road from the south towards Mount Batur, the chief town of the former rajadom of Bangli looks like a nursery for gorgeous flowering shrubs. It comes alive every three days for the big morning market in the central square. To the south of town on the Gianyar road is **Pura Dalem Penunggekan**, a typical example of the many temples for the dead: carved friezes show the nightmarish tortures awaiting sinners in the after-life. On the northern outskirts, the chief temple of the former rajadom of Bangli, **Pura Kehen** is one of Bali's most majestic temples, built upon eight terraces on a wooded hillside. Its fabulously carved gateway, depicting the splayed hands and hideous face of a kala-makara demon, is flanked by elephants, while the forecourt and middle courtyard are shaded by a massive banyan tree with a 'bale kul-kul' (bell tower) entwined within its branches. The courtyard's walls are inset with Chinese porcelain plates, but many have been broken or lost.

Around Lake Batur

The roads from the south climb out of the rice fields of the lowlands, through coffee plantations and orchards at around 600m (2,000ft), eventually thinning out into open pasture. A band of rainforest blocks out the view until you emerge at 1,300m (4,300ft) on the narrow rim of a huge crater (technically a *caldera* or collapsed volcano), 11km (7 miles) across and about 200m (660ft) deep. The pastel blue crescent of Lake Batur takes up the eastern third of the great bowl, and out of the centre soars Mount Batur itself, bare rock streaked with black traces of old lava flows. **Penelokan** ('Place for Looking') can offer a great panorama but it's an ugly village, which is at its worst when enveloped in a cold wet fog and you can't see the view anyway. The peddlers here are the most aggressive in Bali: Balinese travellers have complained about them since long before the arrival of tourists. The height of confusion comes at lunchtime when the tour buses disgorge their passengers at the restaurants, which serve Indonesian buffet lunches.

There's an even better view into the *caldera,* and no fuss, from the road a short way east from Penelokan (heading towards Suter and Rendang, the turnoff for Besakih).

Mount Batur went into an active phase in August 1994, blowing huge puffs of smoke and rocky debris from a new vent on its northwest face. As a result, some of the tracks there were cut; in addition, unsavoury locals are known to harass climbers. Consequently only hikes accompanied by guides from the local guiding cooperative are advised. Travel agencies elsewhere in Bali that specialise in nature/active tours can make arrangements for hikers. A steep zig-zag road winds down to the lake: *Bemos* and motorcycle jockeys are ready to take anyone without transport to **Kedisan**, a lakeside village where you will find a few modest homestays.

On the lake's western shore, reached by a road winding through lava fields, lies **Toyabungkah**, known for its hot springs. They are believed to be both holy and highly therapeutic and are channelled into a public pool – as hot as a steaming bath. You can also enjoy the thermal waters at Toyabungkah's **Natural Hot Springs**, a complex with thermal pools, set in gardens, and spa facilities. A scattering of homestays and rudimentary eating places has now been dwarfed by a big hotel resembling a Chinese palace, with its own fibreglass 'rock' pool fed by hot spring water.

Toyabungkah makes a good base for the two-hour climb (longer in the heat of the day) to the summit of Mount Batur. It's best to start before dawn: Some of the guided parties set out as early as 3.30am. Guides, available locally or at Kintamani, can suggest various longer hikes. **Pura Batur** temple was rebuilt in its present position on the crater rim after a 1926 eruption buried the old site down below. One long street is lined with ugly concrete houses and sheds, relieved by Pura Ulun Danu, the new temple of black volcanic stone started in 1926 that is still being extended. **Kintamani**, adjoining Batur, is brightened up only by its market, on Monday and Thursday mornings.

The road follows on to the north coast, passing close to **Gunung Penulisan**, which is 1,745m (5,725ft) high. A flight of 350 steps takes you to the summit, crowned by Bali's tallest temple, Pura Tegeh Koripan. Traces of stone structures date back to prehistoric times. At the very top, a plain walled enclosure holds a collection of beautiful stone statues and panels portraying gods and rulers, some dating from the 10th and 11th centuries. On a clear day, the views of the mountains and north coast alone make the rather strenuous climb well worth it.

Puru Batur temple

Attendants at Pura Besakih

Gunung Agung

Bali's highest peak, at 3,142m (10,309ft), is also its holiest. Still active today, the volcano erupted in 1963 *(see page 22)* and poured lava down its slopes. Ash covered much of eastern Bali, ruining crops, blocking up the rivers, and causing mudslides that took many lives.

Pura Besakih, known as ◄ 23 Bali's 'mother temple', stands high up on the southwestern slopes of the mountain. From a distance you'll see a forest of black thatched, pagoda-like *meru* roofs rising in tiers above the rice terraces, with the volcano as a backdrop. This was probably a holy place, even in the pre-Hindu era. During more than a thousand years it has evolved into a complex of 86 temples and over 200 shrines. The most important stands in the middle, a shrine with triple lotus thrones representing the three manifestations of Shiva, Hindu god of destruction and reincarnation. Most tour buses arrive at mid-morning and mid-afternoon but no matter when you visit, you will be harassed by hawkers, goaded by guides and ordered by gatekeepers to make donations. Locals don't see this commercial activity as inappropriate; to them, a temple is a place of worship and exchange of material goods in offerings and donations.

There are also guides offering their services to those who want to climb Gunung Agung; only the fit and well-prepared should attempt it, and only in the dry season. The expedition can take as long as six hours and involves a lot of slipping and sliding on stony slopes.

Bedugul

The direct road from Denpasar to Singaraja traverses some of Bali's prettiest hill country, with views of dormant volcanoes and three crater lakes. At about 1,300m (4,300ft), the spring-like climate has made Bedugul – the village has lent its name to the whole area – into something of a mountain retreat. The **Kebun Eka Raya Botanical Gardens** and orchid nurseries are both at their best in the rainy season and make an agreeable place for a stroll or a picnic at any time. This is also the site of **Bali Treetop Adventure Park** (daily 8.30am–6pm; charge). **Bukit Mungsu** market nearby is bright with flowers and superb fruit. There are watersports on **Lake Bratan**, while the lakeside temple of **Pura Ulun Danu** at **Candikuning** is one of Bali's most photogenic (see page 13).

Orchid at the botanical gardens, Candikuning

Pancasari has a variety of cottage-style hotels, and the views of the mountainside towering above **Lake Buyan** in the distance, seen from the championship golf course at **Bali Handara Kosaido Country Club**, are superb. The road winds its way up to the old crater rim above the lake. You will find monkeys congregating wherever you decide to stop and look at the view. Once you've reached the top there's a choice of routes to the north coast. The main road descends by way of bamboo forest and banana plantations direct to Singaraja.

Alternatively, you can take the little-used back road past lakes Buyan and Tamblingan and down through **Munduk** to Seririt *(see page 68)*. The remote hillside villages specialise in growing cloves, and you will see (as well as smell) carpets of the pink buds laid out by the roadside to dry. Munduk is home to an excellent eco-resort, Puri Lumbung *(see page 140)*, and is a terrific base for exploring this beautiful region. The resort organises many activities and co-ordinates inexpensive homestays with local families. In Munduk is the so-called **Pyramid Plastic**, built from melted plastic waste as a reminder of the environmental damage that tourism and industry is causing in Bali. The Munduk waterfalls, accessible at the end of a manageable hike, are spectacular.

THE NORTH COAST

Before the days of flying, most visitors to Bali arrived in the north. The first Dutch military expeditions disembarked near Singaraja, which became the island's administrative capital and the colony's chief port. Now, almost everyone arrives and stays in southern Bali, and only a fraction of them ever take a trip to the north coast, although the journey only takes three hours by road.

There is quite a contrast between the south and north. It is hotter and drier in the north and far less densely populated. The proportion of Muslims is higher; some of the people are descended from traders and immigrants from other islands. There is only a narrow strip of flat land between the mountains and the sea, or in some places none at all. Cactus plants are as common as palm trees and the small area of rice depends on irrigation but produces the island's best grain. The region is also dotted with Bali's local vineyards.

Lacking an airport, losing the status of capital and denied any substantial cash flow from tourism, **Singaraja** hasn't  expanded as much as Denpasar. As can be expected from the former capital, colonial buildings predominate in the port area of **Buleleng** (the original town that gave its name to the northern rajadom) and the old centre. However, there's little here to detain a visitor and no attractive accommodation – for the latter, you would have to travel a short distance from town.

Lovina Beach

The beaches west of Singaraja began to attract travellers in the early 1970s, and simple and fairly inexpensive accommodation was built to house them. Slowly, the number of visitors grew, and the small homestays were converted into larger bungalow-type hotels. Today, tour groups come for short stays and, as everywhere in Bali, standards and prices are steadily

Lovina Beach

Detail of the temple of Pura Beji near Sangsit

going up. Actually, Lovina is not one village but a string of small ones, starting 6km (4 miles) west of Singaraja and continuing for 10km (6 miles) up the coast road. Shops, restaurants and moneychangers are scattered along the busy stretch.

The beach itself is shallow and gently shelving, making it an ideal place for small children. There is calm water on the inside of the reef and good snorkelling over it. Lovina's dark sand is less inviting than the white or golden variety at the southern resorts and gets too hot for bare feet in the middle of the day. Dawn and dusk are the best times for the beach. Dolphins frolic offshore almost every morning – boats will take you out to see them up close. At sunset, the fishermen prepare for a night's work aided by batteries of lights on the boats to attract their catch, while local farmers herd their goats or lead their water buffaloes along the sand.

East of Singaraja

Once clear of the outskirts of the town, at **Sangsit**, look for a turn off the main road (there will be signs), heading towards the sea to the beautiful temple of **Pura Beji**. Decorated with intricate carvings of flowers, animals and monsters, this is the most elaborate and ornate temple in the north.

The road that leads inland for 5km (3 miles) will take you to **Jagaraga**, a village fortified by Jelantik against the Dutch colonialists in 1848 and 1849. The small temple of **Pura Dalem**, on the left-hand side just before you reach the village centre, has some of the strangest carved stone decoration in Bali – and some of the most secular; dating from the 1930s. In one panel, an open-top car carries two European passengers being held up by a man with a gun, while others point up at some aeroplanes – one of them crashing into the sea. Jagaraga is also famous for its dance troupes, which can sometimes be seen in performance here.

Note perfect

It's essential that the craftsmen who manufacture gongs for gamelan orchestras have a musical ear so that they are able to hear whether the sets of gongs are suitable for the five- or seven-tone Balinese scales. The gongmakers are able to ensure the correct note by making adjustments to the mass of metal and its distribution over the surface of the gong.

About 2km (1½ miles) to the south of Jagaraga, **Sawan** has a couple of gongmakers' workshops that supply gamelan orchestras: Another village where the craft is practiced is in Tihingan situated near Klungkung *(see page 53)*. The methods used here are utterly traditional. Bronze is made by melting copper and tin together by heating them in an ancient pot over red-hot charcoal, or else old and broken instruments are recycled. The molten bronze is poured into stone moulds to form rough discs, which are then hammered and heated and hammered again until they finally take the shape of gongs.

Back on the coast road at **Kubutambahan**, in the temple of Pura Maduwe Karang, you'll find a famous carving of a man on a bicycle, its wheels in the form of flowers. To the east, at **Air Sanih** (or Yeh Sanih), you can join local people bathing in the pools fed by a spring and shaded by palm trees.

The often empty coast road continues past Tianyar to
27 ▶ **Tulamben,** renowned for superb snorkelling and diving on
the submerged wreck of the US cargo ship *Liberty,* which
sank here during World War II.

For information on the eastern tip of Bali, *see page 50.*

West of Singaraja

At Dencarik, to the west of Lovina, the road inland climbs
a steep hill before reaching the orange-roofed building of the
Buddhist monastery known as **Brahma Vihara Arama.** This
Thai-style temple, with its bright orange roof and colourful
Buddha images, is strikingly different from the Hindu temples that one typically finds in Bali. A short distance away is
Air Panas Banjar (daily 8am–6pm; charge), where the warm
springs have been piped into a public swimming pool. There
is a smaller and hotter pool, a natural shower and reasonably clean changing rooms.

The market town of **Seririt** is a busy junction with one
road leading across the island to Tabanan and eventually to
Denpasar and the other following the coastal route west-
ward. **Celukanbawang,** 12km (7 miles) from Seririt, is likely
to become an important port if development plans are
realised. After about another 25km (16 miles) of sparsely settled shoreline, you'll come to **Pura Pulaki,** an important temple rebuilt out of grim, black volcanic stone. Traces remain
of older parts of the temple carved out of the cliff face, a natural aggregate of volcanic debris.

A large part of this end of the island has been designated
28 ▶ as the **Bali Barat National Park,** and the road crosses a
small section of it, an area covered with woodland and scrub,
with plenty of grey monkeys. The park encompasses and pro-
tects 760sq km (290 sq miles) of true rainforests, mangrove
swamps and woodlands and is home to over 100 species of
birds (including the endangered Bali Starling), as well as

many indigenous animals. Visitors to the park must be accompanied by an official park guide and issued a park permit. Both guides and permits can be arranged by travel agencies, or at the National Park Headquarters, some 3km (2 miles) south of Gillimanuk.

Labuhan Lalang, on Terima Bay at the western tip of Bali, is the base for boats which make the half-hour journey to Pulau Menjangan (Deer Island). The island is m ainly scrub-covered and only about 3km (2 miles) long, but the coral reefs and clear water here are highly rated among scuba divers.

Across the western tip of Bali, mangrove swamps surround **Gilimanuk**, not much more than one wide street, a few homestays, and the ferry terminal for Java. The silhouette of Gunung Merapi, still an active volcano, is often visible in the mist across the water.

Buddha statue at the Brahma Vihara Arama monastery

WEST OF DENPASAR

Fertile land and high rainfall have brought prosperity to this part of Bali, without the debatable benefits of tourism. In the main towns, you'll find more computer and mobile phone suppliers than souvenir shops. There is very little in the way of accommodation and not much choice when it comes to eating, but the region is rewarding to explore.

29 Mengwi

Just to the northwest of Kapal, there's a major road junction. The right fork goes north to Bedugul *(see page 63)* and Singaraja, but you only have to go about 3km (2 miles) to reach the town of **Mengwi**, where you'll find one of Bali's most beautiful temples and many producers of ceremonial umbrellas.

Pura Taman Ayun, near the centre of town, was built in 1734 and renovated in 1937. It's notable for its double moat. Every morning as well as late in the afternoon, people use the wide outer moat for washing themselves and their clothes. You can circle the outside of the wall that surrounds the inner compound and look in at the cluster of *merus* (pagoda-like, multi-roofed towers). Meru towers may only contain an odd number of roofs, from 3 to 11 tiers.

To the north of Mengwi is **Sangeh Monkey Forest**. The towering 40-m (130-ft) tall Palahlar (*Dipterocarpus trinervis*) trees – often incorrectly assumed to be nutmeg trees – that make up this forest are said to be 300 years old; they are protected for their religious significance. The mischievous resident monkeys engage in their usual business, swinging from branch to branch, and they flock to **Pura Bukit Sari**, the nearby temple, while hawkers swarm around the visitors. Those in the mood to explore should head north from Sangeh, where the road climbs into lovely countryside and rarely visited villages. Eventually it peters out on the slopes of Mount Catur.

Marga

In November 1946, Ngurah Rai and his men were trapped by Dutch forces close to this village, 12km (7 miles) northwest of Mengwi. In an heroic but hopeless last stand they were all killed *(see page 20)*. The battlefield just north of the village is now marked by several memorials. A statue depicts a group of defiant freedom fighters. The Margarana monument is a tall *candi* (or shrine) whose columns carry the symbols of *pancasila*, the five principles of the Indonesian state. Panels record Ngurah Rai's message to the Dutch, demanding their withdrawal and ending with

The entrance to
Pura Luhur Batuku

the words *Sekali Merdeka, Tetap Merdeka* (Once free, always free). Beyond the shrine is a field of memorials to all those who died for the cause of Bali's independence – 1,372 men and women in total. It looks like a cemetery but these are not graves. The museum at the site is worth a visit for the photographs and other relics of the campaign.

North of Marga

If you have reliable transport and a good road map, head further north into the hills for 16km (10 miles) along little-used roads to **Pura Luhur Batukau**, the chief temple of the rajadom of Tabanan, beautifully set amid lush forest. Despite

its ancient appearance, this is a modern reconstruction.

The Tabanan Regency is known as Bali's 'rice bowl' – the most agriculturally productive area on the island with rice fields stretching from the coast to as high as 700m above sea level. From Pura Luhur Batukau take the road east to visit the awesome rice terraces of **Jatiluwih**, which has been a **31** UNESCO World Heritage Site since 2008 for its preservation of traditional Balinese farming techniques. Jatiluwih means 'extraordinary' or 'truly marvellous', which is an apt description for this spellbinding vista.

The rice terraces of Jatiluwih

Tanah Lot

Practically every brochure for Bali shows this exotic sea temple on its rocky islet, often silhouetted against the setting sun. Inevitably, tour buses converge here in late afternoon so everyone can take that same picture. It is 10km (6 miles) down a narrow road from Kediri to the coast, and there can be a long procession of traffic. You might like to plan a dawn visit instead, avoiding at least some of the hawkers **32** who congregate later in the day. **Tanah Lot** is believed to have been founded in the 16th century by the Javanese priest Nirartha, who dedicated it to the sea god. A Japanese-funded project has restored the rock on which the temple stands and cunningly disguised concrete breakwaters. Nothing, however, is done to hold back the commercial tide. Ever more souvenir stands and food stalls cluster as near as they can get and the nearby coast has been developed as a huge, and controversial, resort complex.

The former raja's capital of **Tabanan** goes about its business with few concessions to tourism. The heart of the old town is gone but Tabanan remains a centre for music and dance. **Kerambitan**, just off the main road to the southwest, is a pretty town with two palaces, still the property of a princely family. Today, both palaces, the **Puri Anyar** (New Palace) and the older Puri Gede, act as aristocratic homestays, where guests can experience the traditional hospitality that might have been extended to honoured visitors in the past.

The main road reaches the coast at Soka, with two small beaches and occasional good surfing waves. **Balian Beach** is similar, with informal bungalow accommodation. Experienced surfers head west to **Medewi**, where pleasant new cottage-style hotels face a mostly rocky shore with a small beach. The sea temple of **Pura Rambut Siwi**, off the main road, stands on a black rock overlooking the sandy shore.

Negara, 23km (14 miles) further west, is known for its water-buffalo racing. The sport, which is said to have originated as a ploughing contest, is staged every other Sunday morning between July and November. Tour agencies offer excursions from Kuta, Sanur and the other resort areas.

Racing buffalo

At Negara, each buffalo race is comprised of two pairs of bulls running against each other at speeds of up to 60kmh (40mph) around an erratic 2-km (1.2-mile) track. Festooned with strings of bells, silks and decorative harness, each pair is hitched to a gaily painted wooden chariot, driven by a precariously balanced whip-happy jockey.

LOMBOK

Lombok's scenery and landscape, the people, culture and religion, are all markedly different from that of its neighbour, Bali. There is less rainfall and lower humidity on the smaller island, the beaches are clean and largely undeveloped, and the inland forests are mainly intact. It may be only a 20-minute flight away, two hours on a fast boat or a few hours' ride by the slow car ferry, but it's another world.

Lombok is roughly 70km (43 miles) from north to south and the same distance across. Its great volcano, Gunung Rinjani, is the second highest in Indonesia and dominates the northern half of the island. Most people live on the east–west plain across the middle, on the fertile lands below the mountain range. The far south is arid, with low, scrub-covered hills and eroded valleys, similar to some parts of Australia.

Outrigger on Lombok's Kuta Beach

From a study of their plants and animals, the 19th-century naturalist Alfred Wallace divided the Indonesian islands into a western group, regarded as part of Southeast Asia; and an eastern group, which belonged geographically to Australia/Oceania. He then drew the line between the two through the deep Lombok Strait, separating Bali and Lombok. The division is not so obvious but the basic principle of the 'Wallace Line' as a transitional zone, is still accepted.

For many years, the island of Lombok was the domain of the Sasaks, a people who had come from the Asian mainland by way of Java and Bali. They were animists who revered the spirits they believed to be in the living things and the inanimate objects around them. As Islam spread through the islands (apart from Bali) some people in Lombok adopted it in a version of their own, Wektu Telu, which retained many influences of animism. Today, the majority of people are more or less orthodox Muslims. As you travel about Lombok, you will notice many exotic country mosques with their domes and arabesque arcades, as well as the growing numbers of young women who wear robes and Islamic headscarves.

The first succession of Balinese invasions started in the 18th century. For a while, most of Lombok was governed from Karangasem in Bali. Later, the Balinese province in Lombok became independent, and even attempted to capture Karangasem. The beliefs of the animist-Hindu Balinese and the animist-Muslim Sasaks were not always in conflict and there was much intermarriage. Today, the Balinese minority mainly lives in west Lombok and is influential in commerce and tourism.

At the end of the 19th century, the Dutch took advantage of the conflict raging between the Sasaks and Balinese, joining in on the Sasak side and then taking complete control. After the Japanese occupied Lombok during World War II, the Dutch briefly returned, only to depart again when Indonesia gained independence.

Where to Go in Lombok

The main attractions on Lombok are its laid-back pace, the beautiful, clean beaches, and the natural, unspoilt beauty. Visitors to Lombok are rewarded with the pleasures of the island's relaxed, rustic ways – the sight of water buffaloes and their calves; hens and chicks dashing across your path; and sudden views of the blue sea dotted with sails. Most visitors stay in the hotels around Senggigi beach, or the offshore **Gili Islands**, but the far south also has good beaches and snorkelling.

There are a few notable temples, palaces and other historic sites, and there is a rich culture that needs to be sought out, rather than being on obvious display. The co-existence of Sasak traditions and Balinese-Hindu practices means there are always ceremonies going on – ask at your hotel.

Some villages are renowned for their traditional crafts – basketry, weaving, pottery or carving. For an insight into village life, hire a car or motorbike, or take day trips to the villages and around the enchanting countryside. It's worth inquiring about the timing of local market days, held in the mornings once or twice a week in many towns and villages. Outisde of the towns, the roads are free of traffic, and

Getting Around Lombok

Some organised tours from Senggigi go to a few cultural sites and craft villages, or take you to one of the Gili Islands *(see page 80)* to snorkel or dive. Bemos (minivans; *see page 129*) run from town to town, but rarely outside the densely populated central lowland area. You can arrange to charter them for roughly the price of a rental vehicle per day. The ubiquitous *cidomo* (a pony and cart similar to Bali's *dokar*) is fine for short rides. Taxis outside of Senggigi need to be pre-arranged. Cars are hired at Senggigi and Mataram. Bikes are available for rental, and the mountains are good for hiking in the dry season (June–October).

a prime source of motor power is still the *cidomo*, or pony-drawn carts.

Ampenan, Mataram and Cakranegara

Flights arrive at Selaparang Airport, on the northern outskirts of Lombok's capital, Mataram. The slow ferries from Bali dock at Lembar Harbour, 10km (6 miles) to the south.

Pony express transport

Not so long ago, the old port of Ampenan, the administrative centre of Mataram, and the commercial district of Cakranegara were completely separate. Now they have joined up in an urban sprawl, home to a quarter of a million people. A long, broad avenue links them all and continues to Sweta, the island's transport hub.

The port area of **Ampenan** is crumbling and mostly disused, but the narrow streets of the old town are livelier. Many of the people here are descended from Arab traders – noticeable in the well-attended mosques and the cries of the muezzins in their minarets calling the faithful to prayer.

The **Museum Nusa Tenggara Barat** (Tue–Sun 7am–2pm; charge), south of the centre in Jalan Banjar Tilar Negara, gives an overview of the island's culture, as well as its unique and volatile ecology.

Mataram is the provincial capital of Nusa Tenggara Barat ◀ **35** and has the array of government institutions, as well as tree-lined residential streets with many opulent houses. Monkeys wait by the roadside for handouts as you approach the temple at the top of **Gunung Pengsong**, 6km (4 miles) south.

Cakranegara (or just Cakra – pronounced 'Chakra') grew up around the palace of the Balinese Rajas. Today it is the commercial centre of Lombok. All that remains today of the royal compound is the 1744 **Mayura Water Palace**, the former meeting hall and court of justice standing in the middle of a lake and reached by a causeway guarded by old cannons. This was the scene of a short-lived Balinese victory over Dutch troops in 1894. The result was reversed only weeks later and the Dutch went on to take over the whole island.

Across the street, **Pura Meru**, the biggest temple in Lombok, was built in 1720. It has three meru-topped shrines dedicated to Brahma, Shiva and Vishnu. The huge wooden drums in the outer courtyard are sounded, calling the Hindu community to festivals and ceremonies. Just to the east, **Sweta** buzzes with *bemos*, buses, and pony-powered *cidomos*. The biggest market in Lombok is also here.

Pura Meru, the biggest temple in Lombok

Near the Capital

The hillside gardens and lake at **Narmada**, about 10km (6 miles) east of Cakranegara, were laid out for a 19th-century king, to remind him of Gunung Rinjani and its crater lake when he became

too infirm to make the journey to the real mountain. The resemblance is harder to see now that an extra pool and a rectangular swimming pool have been added.

To the north of Narmada at Lingsar, stands an ecumenical temple, **Pura Lingsar**, intended to bring together people of different religions. The upper compound is reserved for Hindus. The pool in the Wektu Telu temple is the home of big, old holy eels, which can be fed with offerings of boiled eggs sold by vendors at the gate. In another enclosure, the stones, wound in white cloth with a yellow sash, come from Gunung Rinjani and are said to represent ancestral spirits. Chinese Taoists have put mirrors there to repel the malevolent spirits.

At **Suranadi**, in the gardens just east of Lingsar, eggs are on the menu again for the residents of a pond in the Temple of the Holy Eels. Nearby you can swim in a spring-fed pool, or have lunch at the old Dutch-built Suranadi Hotel.

Senggigi Beach and the Gili Islands

Heading north along the coast from Ampenan, look for **Pura Segara**, a sea temple on the shore near the colourful Chinese cemetery. Close by, villagers gather to haul the fishing boats up the beach and help sort the catch.

Pura Batu Bolong straddles an archway on a rock just before Senggigi. This ancient Hindu shrine juts out to sea, and makes a great lookout point for watching the sunset over the Lombok Strait.

36 ▶   The prime place to stay is around **Senggigi Beach**, just north of Batubolong. The beach shelves steeply in places, and the coral reef or rocks can be just below the surface, so it would be advisable that you wear rubber shoes, rather than walk about bare-footed. North of Senggigi, the road passes some of the loveliest coastline in the Indonesian archipelago. At times it climbs to the cliff tops, and then swoops down into breathtaking bays. Tiny fishing villages hide among the palm trees, and the sea is flecked with bright sails.

Instead of the coast road, tours from Senggigi and traffic from Mataram sometimes take the inland route via the **Pusuk Pass**, a winding road through the mountains. The two roads meet at Pemenang, where a side road leads to the small harbour at **Bangsal**, which is the starting point for trips to the

37 ▶   three **Gili Islands** (*gili* means 'island') just offshore. **Gili Air** is nearest, about 3km (2 miles) away. Next is **Gili Meno**, then **Gili Trawangan**, the furthest away at 8km (5 miles) and also the biggest, despite only being 2.5km (1½ miles) long.

With white-sand beaches and coral reefs, the Gilis are favourites of divers, travellers and partygoers. Gili Meno is the quietest of the three, while Gili Trawangan is distinguished as the party island. Here, life is laid-back, with numerous little beachside cafés and bamboo beach bungalows, but no cars, motorbikes or dogs to disturb the peace, although Trawangan now has a wider range of facilities. There are also plenty of dive centres here.

The boats that ply from Bangsal to the islands wait for a full load of 15 to 20 people. In July and August that won't take long, but out of season you can face a delay unless you pay for the empty places or charter a whole boat (fares are low and fixed); be sure to buy tickets from the main building on the beach and avoid the touts or the other makeshift ticket offices, which are operating a scam. Some of the larger hotels on the Gili Islands provide speedboat transfers for guests.

Gunung Rinjani

Mountain Treks

Gunung Rinjani, 3,726m (12,200ft) high, is sacred to both **38** Sasaks and Balinese, who make pilgrimages to its crater lake and hot springs. It attracts hundreds of hikers every year, and two villages in the foothills to the south of Bayan are the most popular starting points for trekking (best in the dry season, from June to November).

A narrow road from the middle of Bayan ascends rapidly to **Batu Koq** and then continues to nearby **Senaru**, where it **39** ends. There are homestays along the road, a few with a *warung* attached, and a restaurant overlooks the valleys, with glimpses of the **Sendang Gile waterfall** below. Guides and porters can be hired by the day or for full treks up the mountain at the Rinjani Trek Centre office.

The main objective of most trekkers is the awesome crater with its beautiful crescent-shaped lake. It's a hard day's walk from Senaru before you reach the rim. The crater itself is

600m (2,000ft) deep, and the steep, slippery scramble down to the lake takes several hours more. Plan at least a three-day expedition – or four if you want to climb to the summit of Rinjani. Those with a lot less time and energy may prefer the half-hour walk in the valley below the restaurant at Senaru to the beautiful waterfalls of Sendang Gile and Tin Kelep.

South and East Lombok

East of Narmada, off the main road that runs through Lombok, there is a cluster of craft villages. Baskets and tablemats from **Loyok** are famous throughout Indonesia. In neighbouring **Rungkang**, they make smooth jet-black pots of all sizes and then weave a fine basket to fit tightly around them, using supple lengths of ultra-thin rattan.

Landscape near Tetebatu

On the southern slopes of Gunung Rinjani, **Tetebatu** is a favourite local retreat, with an old hotel and a couple of homestays overlooking the lush valleys and fields. Here, you can walk to forest waterfalls, while the black monkeys chatter, squeal and swing in the trees.

Labuhan Lombok on the east coast is a hot, dusty, end-of-the-world sort of place, in spite of its picturesque stilt houses. From here, ferries laden with cars, motorbikes and passengers make the crossing eastward to the island of Sumbawa from Kayangan terminal 3km (2 miles) from the village.

At **Sukarara**, to the south of Mataram, almost every house has an old-fashioned back strap loom for weaving the gorgeous *songket* fabric, which mingles gold and silver threads with cotton. **Penujak**, a little further south, produces earthenware pottery in a distinctive, unvarnished style that is exported around the world.

Beleka, east of the market town of Praya, specialises in the craft of intricate basketry. They say that it takes them a week to make a large tablemat. **Rambitan**, to the south just before Kuta, is a traditional type of Sasak village with thatch-and-bamboo houses and tall rice barns but it sees a lot of visitors, and souvenir sellers may well besiege you. **Sade** is similar but smaller. Look for the simple thatch-roofed mosques that you will find in both villages.

In the south, the dry scrub-covered hills slowly give way to semi-desert, before opening up to one of the most stunning coastlines in Indonesia. Best known for some of the area's best surfing, **Kuta Beach** is still far from resembling its namesake in Bali. Most of the time, its white coral sands are largely deserted. Basic accommodation is mostly still in simple cottages, some of which have a modest restaurant.

Located on the sands of nearby **Mandalika Beach** is the Novotel Coralia Resort, designed to resemble a Sasak village, the one upscale resort in the area. If you wish, hotels and local drivers can arrange transport to some of the beautiful, isolated beaches nearby.

The Sunday morning market at the hamlet of Kuta is lively and interesting. Once a year, in February or March, a few days after the second full moon of the year, crowds gather on the beach near the Novotel for the Bau Nyale ceremony. The all-night festival is timed to coincide with the mating of strange worms from the ocean and is steeped in legend.

WHAT TO DO

SPORTS

At the top of the list of Bali's great attractions are its beaches, with the warm waters of the Indian Ocean lapping at the shores. However, the range of active and sports choices is not limited to floating on the waves. The more unusual spectator sports include colourful water buffalo races (also in Lombok) and, to the horror of many visitors, cockfighting, a local favourite in both Bali and Lombok, where it is sometimes carried out as part of religious ceremonies or at festivals, despite the fact that it is against the law.

Watersports

Warm water, gorgeous coral and vivid fish make for great snorkelling over the reefs, especially off the north and east coasts of Bali, Nusa Lembongan and Lombok's offshore Gili Islands *(see page 76)*. Take your own equipment if you have it. Otherwise, many hotels will lend or rent it to you. Superb sites for **scuba diving** include Menjangan, Nusa Penida and Tulamben, off Bali, and Lombok's Gili Islands. Specialist tour operators rent out all the equipment and run courses for complete beginners – make sure that the company you choose is licensed and the instructors are fully qualified, with international certification.

Surfing is a big attraction for surfers the world over, who head for the south and west coasts (Medewi, Canggu and Kuta, down to Uluwatu) in the dry season and the east side (Nusa Dua, Sanur) in the wet months of the year. In most places, local boys with outrigger boats are on hand to transport surfers out

Excursion to Nusa Penida

White-capped waves invite surfers to Bali's shores

beyond the reefs. Difficulty levels range from average to the extreme – there is no 'nursery slope'. The **Rip Curl School of Surf** (tel: 0361-735 858; www.schoolofsurf.com) has lessons ranging from half-a-day to five days and caters for different levels of experience, from beginner to advanced.

At Jimbaran Bay, you can **windsurf** from most of the resort beaches. Equipment can be rented at Kuta, Benoa, Lovina and Sanur. Conditions are not ideal for beginners, though. Falling off into coral is not only painful, it can also harm the fragile ecosystem of the reef.

Whitewater rafting on the Ayung River is also popular. Tour companies like **Sobek** (tel: 0361-768 090; www.balisobek.com) and **Bali Adventure Tours** (tel: 0361-721 480; www.baliadventuretours.com) will pick you up at your hotel, then take you to the launch point on the Ayung river near Ubud and provide you with the necessary equipment for an exhilarating trip.

On Dry Land

Golf courses at Nusa Dua, Pecatu on the Bukit, Nirwana near Tanah Lot, and up in the mountains at the Bali Handara Kosaido Country Club are all top-class, staging tournaments, which bring some of the world's best players. There's a 9-hole course at Sanur, and at Lombok there is the 18-hole Suranadi course. Many hotels offer their own **tennis** courts, some floodlit for evening use. As the sun starts to set, informal soccer and volleyball games between visitors and locals begin on the beach at Kuta, Tuban and Legian.

Walking and **cycling** in the countryside are among the great pleasures of Bali. Don't start at the southern resorts, which are a long way from the best scenery, but begin instead up in the hills, where it's cooler. In Ubud, the Bina Wisata Information Centre or your hotel can give you information on walks along the Campuan Ridge, or through picturesque rice fields. Bookstores in Ubud sell detailed maps including *Bali Pathfinder* and *Ubud Surroundings* that will help guide you along country pathways. Victor Mason's popular **Bali Bird Walks** (tel: 0361-975 009) includes lunch, water and use of binoculars. At Munduk, in the mountains southwest of Lovina, **Puri Lumbung Cottages** *(see page 140)* offers a programme of walks and treks.

The more arduous and serious mountain **treks** include climbing Gunung Batur – a trek of several hours (minimum of two hours up) – and the crater rim and lake of Gunung Rinjani (on Lombok), which demands at least three days to complete.

Massage, both relaxing and therapeutic, is a Balinese

Cycling downhill

Tour companies such as Sobek and Bali Adventure Tours *(see page 86 for contact details)* offer a variety of cycling (and trekking) tours. One of the more popular cycling trips is the scenic downhill trail starting from Gunung Batur.

tradition that many visitors have come to enjoy. The beaches are filled with men and women offering reasonably good massage at prices that are very low. Many areas have excellent massage centres or spas that offer very professional massage treatment, including mineral baths, all starting at approximately US$15; hotels and resorts offer similar treatment in more pampering surroundings for considerably more money.

Spectator Sports

Regular **buffalo races** are held at Negara in western Bali, and in Lombok, with the lumbering beasts pulling decorated carts at surprising speeds of up to 60kmh (40mph). **Kite-flying** is a local obsession at Sanur and on the windswept Bukit Peninsula. You can buy beautiful, hand-painted kites at stands or from hawkers at Sanur and also at Kuta.

In Lombok, **ritual fights** long ago took the place of war. The Balinese and Sasaks hurl packets of cooked rice at each other in the October or November *perang ketopaq* festival. Large crowds gather regularly in villages in Lombok to watch *peresehan* contests, in which men armed with rattan canes and leather shields lash at each other until the referee declares one of them the victor.

Take Care

The sea may look perfect for swimming, but it needs to be approached with caution. Rocks, coral and sudden deep holes can lie concealed just below the water, especially at low tide. Sharp pieces of coral are a hazard almost everywhere, so it's worth wearing rubber shoes whenever you enter the water. Waves breaking over reefs are especially dangerous: only swim or snorkel there in calm conditions. Take local advice, only swim between the marker flags, don't swim or surf alone, and acknowledge your limitations.

ENTERTAINMENT

Traditional Music, Puppetry and Dance Performances

The sound of music in Bali can be the hypnotic tones of the *gamelan* orchestra, or the alluring call of the disco beat in the clubs of Kuta or Seminyak, where the action begins at midnight and lasts until dawn. In the rest of the resort areas, the nightlife is on a much smaller scale.

Bali's own celebrated culture of dance and drama flourishes on two levels: for the visitors and for locals themselves. Ask at hotels, travel agencies, and tourist

Shadow puppet in Denpasar

information offices to find out what is scheduled during your stay. They'll probably point you towards some of the commercial performances put on in several villages, mostly in the Ubud area. Tickets (including transport) are sold at the tourist office in Ubud, by touts in the street, and by many of the tour operators. Increasingly, the culture is packaged and brought to you in shows staged at hotels. Some of these are of a very high standard, since dedicated dancers and musicians usually give their best. But inevitably the atmosphere is different when they are performing for untutored tourists eating dinner, rather than for an expert village audience – and above all for their gods.

Drama and dance students will think that they've gone to heaven when they see the unique temple ceremonies. If you are invited, be prepared to wait. Starting times are highly elastic and then some events will last for many hours.

Many of the dances of Bali are also performed in western Lombok, either for the Balinese community there or for the tourists at Senggigi hotels. Lombok also has its own special dances, which are rarely staged commercially. The *gandrung* dance resembles Bali's *joged*, in that a girl picks a male partner from the audience. Another group of dances is based on romantic legends from Sasak mythology. Western-style nightlife is limited to Senggigi, where hotels run discos and local groups play in the bar-restaurants.

Gamelan

Impossible to describe, unmistakable once you have heard it, the bell-like sound of a *gamelan* orchestra is Bali's musical heartbeat. You'll hear the players practising when you stroll through a village, or see them in their matching shirts and sarongs, loading their instruments onto the back of a truck to set off for an engagement somewhere. A gamelan orchestra will accompany most of the dance performances at the hotels as well as at every temple festival. There must be tens of thousands of such groups, all different. Each banjar has at least one, with its own unique collection of valuable instruments – gongs, metallophones (metal versions of xylophones), drums, cymbals and flutes. They are tuned to five- or seven-note 'scales', instead of the Western octave. The music is extremely complex – all the more so because performances, which continue for many hours, entail constant interplays of improvisation on the part of musicians.

The *gamelan* came to Bali from Java and still flourishes there, but after four centuries of separation it has evolved differently and taken on its own character.

Puppet shadow plays, or *wayang kulit* (leather puppet), are not so often put on for tourists – the plots are too complex and the plays last too long (up to 4 hours) for foreign consumption. A temple ceremony may give you a chance to join the audience for a while.

Dances of Bali

Gamelan musicians play a wide array of instruments.

Legong: This is the most popular dance with visitors and is performed by three young girls: two principal dancers, the legongs, no more than 12 or 13 years old, and an attendant. Each is exquisitely dressed in glittering gold-leafed fabrics and wears a gilded leather headdress embellished with fresh frangipani flowers. The usual version *(legong kraton)* is the tale of a king and the princess he has abducted, performed by the two principals who, using various hand and facial gestures, portray the attempted seduction.

Kecak: Inspired in the 1920s by a ritual trance-dance which is called *sanghyang*. Up to 150 men in sarongs crouch in concentric circles around a flickering lamp and chant hypnotically while the story is acted out in the centre of the circle. Taken from the Hindu epic *Ramayana* and popularly known as 'Monkey Dance', it concerns Rama and the monkey armies led by Hanuman.

Panyembrama: Girls carrying trays of flower petals open the evening by scattering the petals over the stage as a symbol of welcome. At temple ceremonies the original dance called *pendet* is performed mostly by older women to welcome the gods.

Kecak dance at Pura Luhur Uluwatu on the Bukit peninsula

Janger: Twelve boys and twelve girls in groups of six form a square, the girls kneeling and swaying together to the music like reeds in the wind. The boys, wearing false moustaches, try to impress the girls as they strut like fighting roosters.

Joged: A whole family of dances shares this name, performed to the music of an orchestra of bamboo xylophones, flutes, drums, cymbals and gongs. A young woman dances alone at first and then taps members of the audience in turn with her fan to dance with her. Try as they may to flirt or show off, she easily slips away from their advances. Few Westerners look anything but clumsy in comparison but it's more of a social than artistic dance.

Barong: A mythical lion-like animal, the *barong* is covered in long hair and little mirrors. Animated by two men, it fights against the evil Rangda, queen of the witches. As she advances on her victims she holds a white cloth as a magical weapon in her long claw-like fingernails; her eyes bulge, her fangs flash, and flames flicker from her tongue. Allies of the barong, men each carrying a *kris,* try to attack Rangda but she puts them under a spell. In a trance, they turn the daggers on themselves. Only the reappearance of the barong saves them. In daily performances for visitors (each morning at Batubulan, for instance) the trances are inevitably simulated. Late at night in a village, however, you would see the wild-eyed men in a genuine frenzy or collapsing at the climax into unconsciousness, until revived by priests who sprinkle them with holy water.

Other Dances: Other performances you might see include scenes from the *Ramayana,* staged as a dance-drama. These may well be a showcase for fine dancing, gorgeous costumes and the full *gamelan* orchestra. In the *topeng,* the dancers are masked, which means that they can convey character and emotion through movement alone. The stories behind the dances are taken from Balinese history and mythology.

Kebyar is the name of a group of solo dances of which the best known are performed by a soloist, using mostly the upper body. *Baris* is a vehicle for a soloist or groups of male dancers to display their command of technique, conveying a great range of emotions of a warrior.

Days and Dates

The Balinese pawukon calendar consists of 30 weeks *(wuku)* of seven days each. Confusingly superimposed on that are other 'weeks', which can be anything from one to ten days. Every 210 days comes the holiday **Galungan**, a 5-day festival for the divine ancestors, which always begins on a Wednesday. Tall bamboo poles, known as 'penjor', bearing bright flowers and palm leaf decorations stand at the gate of each house. It is believed that ancestral spirits visit the homes of their descendants and are presented offerings. Ten days later on **Kuningan** everyone acknowledges the blessings of the gods and ancestors.

SHOPPING

Bali produces a wide range of crafts in every medium. Most of the decorative arts and crafts originally had a religious connection, as temple embellishments, offerings or ceremonial dress. The land yielded plenty to eat without the need to work all day, every day, so people had time to create objects of beauty. The tradition continues, although production has been multiplied by the demand for souvenirs and export. Some village craft shops have workshops attached, or you can watch the carvers, painters or weavers in the adjoining compound.

In the past, nothing was expected to last: the climate and insects saw to that. So hardly anything is very old – 'Antiques Made to Order' shop signs give the game away.

Wood carvings: Dozens of villages in Bali devote themselves to the island's biggest craft business; the village of Mas

Traditional *ikat* fabric

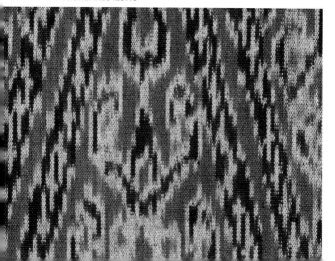

(see page 40) is the best-known, with hundreds of carvers and countless shops. Behind the scenes – but you may be invited for a visit – fathers pass on their skills to

Avoid old cash

Don't accept worn *rupiah* bills. You may have difficulty passing them on.

their sons, while the women do the polishing or painting. The best carvings are superb sculptures, but even the simplest, cheapest article can make an appealing souvenir. Among the massed garuda birds and masks, you're bound to find something beautiful.

The sign 'Parasite Carvings' might puzzle you. A new idea, imported from the West, is to take the strange growths that occur on tree trunks and carve them into a witty or grotesque design, using the natural shape.

Jewellery: The village of Celuk *(see page 39)* has specialised in producing silver and gold jewellery for centuries, so when tourism arrived, its position on the Denpasar-Ubud road was ideal. Dozens of tour buses stop at the big shops but there are also many little workshops worth visiting. The smiths can produce any style, from intricate filigree work to simple bracelets. You don't have to go to Celuk though, since every resort area has its share of shops. Silver should bear the '925' stamp of sterling silver.

Clothes and Fabrics: Bali is a huge bargain basement for a selection of beachwear, casual clothing and, at a higher price but still excellent value, fashion designs. For the biggest choice of shops go to Kuta, and look for dresses, shirts, sarongs and cover-ups in traditional *batik* fabric.

Batik dyeing technique uses hot wax to draw or stamp a design on cloth before dipping it in the dye, so that the waxed areas are left undyed. The process can be repeated a number of times for greater complexity. Java is the source of the batik for dresses and sarongs sold in fashion shops;

Balinese versions are usually much coarser. Hawkers will swear that their dress lengths of cheap printed cotton are batik. It's easy to tell that they are not: printed patterns don't penetrate fully to the other side, while the real batik will show thin veins of colour where the dye runs along tiny cracks in the wax (printed versions may try to simulate this). Real batik is always *much* more expensive. Used batik sarongs are highly prized, as their patterns are often no longer produced. Used batik can be purchased at a number of textile shops in Kuta, Ubud and Denpasar.

Endek or **ikat** fabrics, using warp or weft threads dyed in patterns before weaving, come from Bali as well as other Indonesian islands. In Bali, only the weavers of Tenganan Pageringsingan make *geringsing,* or double *ikat,* using pattern-dyed threads for both warp and weft. The genuine fabric is

Bargaining

Love it or loathe it, there's no escape unless you go to a modern fixed-price store or supermarket. Otherwise, practically every purchase, large or trivial, will be the subject of a session of haggling. Here are a few suggestions to make the process easier:

• If possible, have some idea of the going rate before you start. Identical items may be offered for Rp18,000 in one place and Rp55,000 in another. Hotel shops tend to be the most expensive, but the best of them have genuine treasures you won't find anywhere else.

• You'll do best if you are not part of a group or are without a guide-driver, since he gets a percentage added to the price.

• Do not mention a price first. Instead, put the onus on the seller to name a price first.

• If you automatically offer half that figure – the beginner's usual mistake – you've already lost the contest. The seller might have accepted one-fifth, or less, but now you will never know.

justifiably expensive – be wary of fakes. You can find bold, primitive examples of *ikat* cloth, especially from Indonesian islands such as Sumba, Flores and Timor, in good textile shops.

Paintings: If you want to purchase a unique work of art, you'll need to study the field. Visit the major collections to judge the standard of the best paintings, especially the Neka Art Museum and Museum Puri Lukisan in Ubud *(see page 42)* as well as the Taman Budaya

A Lombok potter crafts one of the local souvenirs by hand

Art Centre in Denpasar *(see page 38)*. Don't just assume that a high price guarantees original work.

And More... Look for the **basketry** from Bona, leather wayang *kulit* **leather puppets** from Sukawati and decorative **umbrellas** on roadside stalls east of Klungkung.

Shops take advantage of the tourist traffic to sell the products of other islands, too – **embroidery** and *songket* **fabrics** from Sumatra, **primitive art** from Irian Jaya and **silver** from Sulawesi.

Lombok: Craft skills in Lombok tend to be devoted to household objects that have a natural functional beauty. Look for the delicate, tightly woven basketware, whether in mats, boxes, bowls and bags, or the common Lombok souvenir of a model rice-barn. Carved or painted wooden boxes to store spices, tobacco or jewellery are attractive. Simple red pottery comes from Penujak; black pots from Rungkang are bound in intricately woven baskets.

Necessities: Some supermarkets and convenience stores in Denpasar, such as Tiara Dewata, on Jalan Jenderal Sutoyo, have books, shoes, cosmetics and even a playground for children and a swimming pool. Discovery Mall is the huge shopping centre in Tuban, while others can be found in Kuta, Nusa Dua, Ubud and Senggigi. In most tourist areas, modern grocery shops, with big red 'K' signs (Circle K), as well as Minimart, are open 24 hours a day and sell all kinds of necessities.

BALI FOR CHILDREN

The Balinese treasure their children and yours will get the same treatment. Some resorts run children's activity programmes during the day, show videos in the early evening and offer a babysitting service when you want to go off on your own. In *losmen* and homestay accommodation, the children of the owner's family will probably want to make friends and the older girls may offer to babysit.

Children will, of course, revel in the hotel pools and the beaches, the slides at the Waterbom park in Tuban and, when the conditions are right, they can learn to snorkel, sail and windsurf. The well-planned **Taman Burung Bali Bird Park** (daily 9am–5.30pm; charge), with over a hundred species of birds, is always a hit with children. At Bedugal's **Bali Treetop Adventure Park** (daily 8.30am–6pm; charge), children and adults can venture from tree to tree through suspended bridges, spider nets, Tarzan jumps and flying foxes.

Surfing courses are available

Festival Calendar

Most festivals are fixed by calendars different from the Western version *(see page 93)*, so they change each year. Look for the Bali Government Office of Tourism's annual Calendar of Events.

March or April *Nyepi: Bali's Day of Silence* occurs on the day that follows the dark moon of the spring equinox. There are no flights in or out of Bali, shops are closed, streets are deserted and no lights are switched on. The days before Nyepi are filled with activity. Religious objects are taken in lavish processions from the temples to sacred springs or the sea for purification. Exciting street processions take place on the night before Nyepi as the evil spirits are driven away with gongs, drums, cymbals, firecrackers and huge papier-mâché monsters known as 'ogoh-ogoh'.

Mid-June–mid-July *Bali Arts Festival:* A month-long fiesta of Balinese and Indonesian artistic traditions and culture, at the Taman Budaya Art Centre and in the various Regency capitals

June or July *Mekare-kare Pandan Fight:* The 'mekare-kare' fight, between the young men of the village of Tenganan, uses prickly pandanus leaf whips.

July *Bali Kite Festival, Padanggalak:* Staged in Sanur, traditional giant kites are made and flown competitively by teams from different villages.

July–October *Negara Bull Races:* Said to have originated as a simple ploughing competition, this extraordinary contest, held every other Sunday, features Bali's sleekest, most handsome water buffalo.

17 August *Indonesian Independence Day:* Celebrated with flags, processions, dancing and other merry-making.

September *Kuta Karnival:* Ten days of festivities, featuring live music, performing arts, contests, beach games, food festivals and exhibitions.

October *Ubud Writers & Readers Festival:* This annual event attracts writers and lovers of literature from all over the globe. The *Nusa Dua Festival* presents some of Bali and Indonesia's finest performing arts.

Galungan. During the *Galungan festival*, held every 210 days according to the Balinese calendar, the temples in Bali are beautifully decorated, while the streets are lined with 'penjor', gracefully arching bamboo poles, festooned with palm fronds and offerings.

EATING OUT

The countless places to eat in Bali fall into three broad categories: the hotels, the restaurants aimed at foreign visitors, and those intended mainly for the Balinese. Each type is certainly worth trying.

The choice in Lombok is more limited but there are some very good restaurants in Senggigi and out on the Gilis, and you can also find tasty local dishes in the *warungs* and city restaurants. The word *lombok* actually means 'chilli pepper', so watch out for it in the local dishes.

WHERE TO EAT

Hotels usually have at least one restaurant. In big resorts, there may be a whole range, offering Japanese or Chinese food, and 'international' and Indonesian dishes, too. Some places can be dull, while some are excellent, with prices to match.

Many hotels regularly stage theme buffet nights: seafood, a barbecue or a *Pasar Malam* (Night Market), where a variety of enticing food stalls tempt you with dishes from all round the Pacific region, or from every Southeast Asian nation. A good *rijsttafel* (Dutch for rice table), comprising a banquet of side dishes accompanying rice, is a fine way to experience a range of cooking in the Indonesian tradition. Compare the prices of these hotel events – often they include entertainment and can be excellent value and are also a good way to sample a variety of different styles of cooking.

The majority of eating places in Indonesia used to be run by Chinese (many still are today) and the food is a

Colonial invention

Dutch colonials invented *rijsttafel* as a way to sample Indonesian cuisine.

hybrid. *Nasi goreng*, which consists of fried rice, lightly spiced with chillis and garlic and combined with some finely chopped vegetables and a little meat, chicken, or a few shrimps – menus usually list the options – is practically the national dish. *Nasi rames* is white rice with vegetable and meat dishes; *bak mie goreng* means similar combinations but based on rice-flour noodles. In *nasi campur* the rice is topped with meat, vegetables and egg. Instead of bread you'll get *krupuk*, large deep-fried crackers, which accompany most Indonesian meals.

Spices and flavours may be toned down to the tastes of foreigners. Ask for dishes to be *pedas* (spicy) if that is what you want. Some places respond by bringing you a bottle of *sambal*, ultra-hot chilli, lime and prawn paste.

If you want a cheaper meal you can choose between one of the street stalls *(warung)*, a dining room *(rumah makan)* or a more modest restaurant serving standard Indonesian fare.

Nasi campur for sale at Gianyar food market

Bebek betutu accompaniments

WHAT TO EAT

When the numbers of tourists began to build up, so did the demand for alternatives to the typical Indonesian diet, starting with the Australians, who called for 'good Aussie tucker' (still to be found in Kuta). Hindus are not supposed to eat beef, but there is no apparent reluctance to serve beef to others, so you can order a pretty good steak, perhaps imported from New Zealand or Australia. Restaurants of many different ethnicities have also sprung up.

The 'seafood market' concept arrived in Bali some time ago – you make your choice from a big display and hand it over to be cooked. Giant prawns and lobster come at the top of the price list, charged per 100 grams, so keep an eye on the cost or the bill can be quite a shock. The many beachside restaurants at Jimbaran use this system.

Bali has its own fast foods, too: *pisang goreng*, crispy fried banana fritters and *saté* – mini-kebabs of tender meat, prawns or fish cooked over charcoal and served with a squeeze of lime juice and peanut sauce. The crunchy fried dragonflies find fewer foreign takers.

Balinese Dishes

Bali's specialities are mainly reserved for festivals. Simplified versions turn up on a few restaurant menus, and big hotel kitchens sometimes show off their skills by including Balinese dishes in their buffet events. The **Bumbu Bali** restaurant, at

Tanjung Benoa *(see page 109)*, serves excellent traditional Balinese dishes and offers classes at its cooking school.

At all the big temple ceremonies or family celebrations you will find *lawar*, in which cooked and finely chopped meat of a pig or chicken, steamed vegetables, grated coconut, plenty of garlic, shallots, hot red chillis and fresh spices are subtly combined by an expert. Raw minced meat, blood and lime juice are mixed in before serving the colourful *lawar* on a banana leaf. A *lawar* on a hotel buffet usually omits the raw meat and blood.

The local ducks may appear on the table, in the form of *bebek betutu*, in which they are rubbed and stuffed with a fiery mixture of chillis, garlic and spices. Sometimes, a whole duck is wrapped in layers of banana leaves before being cooked slowly in a clay oven. Thus it is steamed, roasted and smoked simultaneously and the meat should

A Table with a View

Bali offers the chance for gourmet meals that dreams are made of, served in settings that are beyond belief and at prices that are reasonable by standards in the West. You'll find a table with one of the island's most memorable views at the **Four Seasons Sayan**; nearby, the **Amandari**'s view is just a little less dramatic, but its Indonesian-style dishes are perfection. For a vista of sea and sky, try **Di Mare** at Karma Kandara on the Bukit, or the exclusive **Amankila**'s terrace restaurants perched on a cliff near Candidasa. The Restaurant at the **Damai Lovina Villas**, on a hill overlooking the sea near Lovina, offers a setting straight out of paradise, and an exquisite 'Nouvelle Indonesian' menu unlike anything else found on Bali. Finally, for those on an under US$15 a meal budget, the balcony of the **Indus** restaurant, overlooking a river gorge at the edge of Ubud, is a sure bet for a romantic meal, and the Indus will even shuttle you over from the Casa Luna in Ubud for free.

practically be falling off the bones. Restaurant versions can be disappointing. The **Dirty Duck** restaurant in Ubud give you an idea of what a whole fried Balinese duck is like – you pull the meat off the bones with your fingers.

In the rest of Indonesia, most people are Muslims and don't eat pork. In Bali, the reverse applies: for Hindus, pork is permitted. *Babi guling*, spit-roasted pig is a rare luxury for large feasts and celebrations – the centrepiece of many a banquet. Once it's been stuffed with finely chopped chillis, garlic, ginger and spices, the pig is slowly roasted over an open fire until it's cooked through and the skin is crisp. Next to the Ubud Palace you'll find **Ibu Oka**, an informal lunch place where Balinese and foreigners alike crowd in to enjoy roast pork. It's renowned as being the best babi guling eatery in Bali.

When dining with Balinese, help yourself generously to rice, then take just a little from side dishes. Wait to be asked

Satay grilling by the roadside, Denpasar

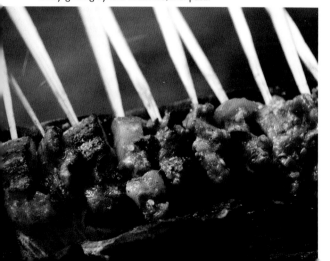

by your host to start eating
or drinking. The left hand is
considered to be unclean, so
when passing food or eating
with your fingers use the
right hand.

Desserts

For dessert, your best bets
are the fresh fruit: mangoes,
bananas, passion-fruit, mandarin oranges and the less
familiar *rambutan* (small,

Balinese sweets at Ubud market

red and hairy), rose apple, custard apple and *salak* (or snake-
fruit, a fruit that is covered in hard brown scales). Black rice
pudding is just that – boiled black rice served with sweetened
coconut milk. Pancakes have caught on here – try them: they
are usually served with fresh pineapple and banana.

Drinks

Oranges, bananas, pineapples and some tropical fruits are
pulped into delicious juices, but make sure you are buying
from a hygienic source. You will find bottled water and bottled drinks sold everywhere in Bali; even at the smallest food
stall. A pot of not-too-strong tea without milk makes a good
accompaniment to a typical Indonesian meal. So, too, does
the good local beer.

The best Balinese rice wine, *brem*, is usually sweet and
oxidized; it's the base of a lot of fruit cocktails and especially
nice with lime and ice. Hatten Rosé wine is among the best
from local Balinese vineyards, and is very inexpensive.
Imported beers, spirits and wines are readily available, but
prices are excessive due to a high customs and excise tax.
Bintang is the most popular local beer.

TO HELP YOU ORDER

I would like...	**Saya ingin...**

beer	**bir**	milk	**susu**
bread	**roti**	orange juice	**air jeruk**
breakfast	**sarapan pagi**	pepper	**merica**
butter	**mentega**	salt	**garam**
coffee	**kopi**	sugar	**gula**
dinner	**makan malam**	tea	**teh**
fruit	**buah-buahan**	the menu	**daftar makanan**
ice cream	**es krim**	water	**air**
lunch	**makan siang**	wine	**anggur**

...AND READ THE MENU

asam manis	sweet and sour	**kare**	curry (mild)
ayam	chicken	**kecap**	soy sauce
babi	pork	**kelapa**	coconut
babi guling	roast pig	**kentang**	potato
bak mie	noodles	**kepiting**	crab
bebek betutu	roast smoked duck	**krupuk**	prawn- or fish-flavoured rice crackers
bistik	steak		
bubur	rice porridge	**manggis**	mangosteen
capcai	stir-fried vegetables	**markisa**	passionfruit
		mie	noodles
gado gado	vegetables and peanut sauce	**nanas**	pineappple
		nasi putih	plain rice (steamed)
goreng	fried	**soto**	soup
ikan	fish	**telur**	egg
kambing	goat	**udang**	shrimp (prawn)

PLACES TO EAT

We have used the following symbols to give an idea of the price for a starter, main course and dessert, per person. A charge is often added for service and tax. This is not consistent, but 21 percent is typical:

$$$$$ over $30 $$$$ $20–30
$$$ $10–20 $$ $6–10 $ below $6

SOUTHERN BALI

JIMBARAN BEACH

$$$–$$$$ Jimbaran Beach is lined with restaurants with tables along the sands serving freshly cooked fish and seafood. It's part of the Bali experience to taxi here before sunset, choose a restaurant, choose a fish (price is by weight) and dine watching the sunset, with the waves almost at your feet. A madhouse in high season, but memorable. Some places take credit cards.

KUTA/LEGIAN

Aromas $$$ *Jalan Legian, tel: 0361-751 003.* Open daily 8am–10pm; more extensive menu at dinner. The best vegetarian restaurant in Bali, this tranquil garden oasis offers an inventive and always excellent international range of tasty vegetarian choices served in generous portions. Mostly organically grown ingredients; great fruit and veggie juices. Credit cards.

Made's Warung 1 $$ *Jalan Pantai Kuta, tel: 0361-755 297.* Open daily 9am–midnight. A Kuta institution for years, this is a small busy place where tables are shared, and both the Indonesian and Western food is above average. Major credit cards.

TJ's Mexican $$$ *Poppies Gang, tel: 0361-751 093.* Open daily 8am–11.30pm. Great Mexican food, including stylish California-inventions such as wraps filled with red curried shrimp or yogurt and beans. Large portions, attractive garden setting. Credit cards.

SEMINYAK

Gateway of India $$ *Jalan Abimanyu, tel: 0361-732 940*. Open daily for lunch and dinner. Serves authentic northern Indian food, with a tandoori oven in operation at dinner. Delicious curries served with rice or a variety of breads. A must-try starter is the lamb or chicken *kathi* roll, a sort of pancake with a spicy filling. Very casual dining. Branches in Kuta (Jalan Pantai Kuta 11, tel: 754 463) and Sanur (Jalan Danau Tamblingan 103, tel: 281 579).

Ku De Ta $$$$$ *Jalan Laksmana, tel: 0361-736 969*. Open daily for breakfast, lunch and dinner. Stunning beachside location and stylish waiters bring flair to the Seminyak dining scene. The creative Western dishes with Asian touches has earned rave reviews from the local media. Major credit cards.

La Lucciola $$$$ *Jalan Petitenget, tel: 0361-261 047*. Open daily 8.30am–midnight. With terraces right on a beautiful stretch of beach, this is a place to come for a romantic, sunset dinner. The pasta and sauces are fresh and lively. Roasted pork and lamb dishes are recommended. Major credit cards.

Made's Warung 2 $$$ *Jalan Raya Seminyak, tel: 0361-732 130*. Open daily 9am–midnight. Spacious, upscale branch of Made's Warung, with foreign and local clientele enjoying the fabulous house specials: nasi campur, fresh snapper and chicken stuffed with mushrooms in soya/ginger sauce. Major credit cards.

Métis $$$$$ *Jalan Petitenget 6, tel: 0361-737 888*. Open Mon–Sat for lunch and daily for dinner. Delicious French Mediterranean cuisine is on offer here. Signature dishes include the pan-seared hot foie gras with port and raspberry reduction, morello cherry and roasted apple.

Sardine $$$$$ *Jalan Petitenget, tel: 0361-738 202*. Open daily for dinner. This bamboo pavilion in the rice fields features a polished bamboo bar and a gourmet menu emphasising fresh fish and seafood, as well as some meat and vegetarian dishes. Guests are guaranteed a gorgeous rural view.

Veranda $$ *Jalan Raya Seminyak, 31B, tel: 0361-732 685.* This award-winning restaurant deserves a visit. Excellent international cuisine at sensible prices is served here, alongside some Swedish favourites, such as meatballs with mashed potato and Lingonberry jam. Their Gravlax is perfect. Major credit cards.

NUSA DUA/BENOA

Bumbu Bali $$$ *Benoa Village, tel: 0361-774 502, www.bali food.com.* Open daily 11am–11pm. This restaurant is famous for a large menu of authentic, beautifully presented Balinese dishes. Seafood and duck in banana leaf lead the specialities. Cooking classes offered. Free transport from Nusa Dua hotels; worth a trip from Kuta and Sanur. Major credit cards.

SANUR

Café Batujimbar $$$ *Jalan D. Tamblingan, tel: 0361-287 374.* Open Mon–Sat 7am–11pm, Sun 7am–4pm. Indonesian and California/international dishes, all inventively prepared. Great salads and veggies from the restaurant's own farm; breads and cakes from in-house bakery. Informal atmosphere. Spicy Manadonese curried fish especially recommended. Major credit cards.

Tanjung Sari $$$$ *Tanjung Sari Hotel, Jalan D. Tamblingan, tel: 0361-288 441.* Open daily 7pm–midnight. A romantic beachside pavilion serving mainly Indonesian-style, beautifully presented meals. The Saturday evening traditional Dutch-Indonesian *rijstaffel* buffet includes one of the best classical dance performances on Bali. Major credit cards.

UBUD AND VICINITY

Ary's Warung $$$–$$$$ *Jalan Raya, tel: 0361-975 053.* Open daily 7.30am–1am. Downtown Ubud's most stylish restaurant offers an excellent Western menu of fish, lamb and duck dishes, savoury crêpes and many hard-to-find Indonesian specialities. At the café/bar are inventive tropical alcoholic and non-alcoholic drinks: honey-lime-ginger is a favourite. Major credit cards.

Batan Waru Kafé $$$ *Jalan Sri, tel: 0361-977 528*. Open daily 8am–11pm. Delicious Indonesian and Western cuisine, refreshing drinks and tasty desserts in big portions are served here. Excellent value for money. Ask for a table at the back as it's quieter.

Café Lotus $$ *Jalan Raya, tel: 0361-975 660*. Open daily 8am–11pm. A magical setting beside a lotus pond and dramatic temple. The menu is Indonesian/international. Major credit cards.

Café Wayan $$ *Monkey Forest Road, tel: 0361-975 063*. Open daily 10am–10pm. Tables and dining pavilions dot a vast garden; the food is a mix of Western and Indonesian. The cakes, from the café's own bakery, are delicious. Cash only.

Casa Luna $$$ *Jalan Raya, tel: 0361-973 283*. Open daily 7.30am–11pm. With a California/international/Indonesian menu, and its own bakery, this is a busy place and a favourite meeting point for travellers. Credit cards.

Dirty Duck Diner (Bebek Bengil) $$$ *Jalan Hanuman, Padang Tegal, tel: 0361-975 489*. Open daily 8am–11pm. This is a fashionable open-air café set in the rice fields, with a spectacular view of Mount Agung. The portions are on the small side, but highly recommended is its crispy duck (*bebek betutu*). Another branch on Jalan Wanara Wana (Monkey Forest Road).

Ibu Rai $$ *Monkey Forest Road, tel: 0361-975 066*. Open daily 7am–11pm. A picturesque thatch-roofed pavilion, great for people-watching, where you'll find tasty Indonesian and Western cuisine served in big portions at low prices. Daily fresh fish specials. Cash only.

Indus $$$ *Campuhan, tel: 0361-977 684*. Open daily 7.30am–11pm. In a dramatic setting overlooking the Campuhan gorge and sharing management with the popular Casa Luna, this is a romantic spot for a wonderful meal. Balinese paella and spiced sweet potato soup head the menu of Balinese/California/international choices. Very reasonable prices. Free shuttle from Casa Luna on Jalan Raya in downtown Ubud. Credit cards.

CANDIDASA

Kafé Watergarden $$$–$$$$ *Jalan Raya Candidasa, tel: 0363-41540.* Open daily for breakfast, lunch and dinner. The Asian and European cuisine is reliably good at this open-air place.

Toke $$$ *Jalan Raya Candidasa; tel: 0363-41991.* Open daily for lunch and dinner. The menu presents Western, Balinese and Indian food, with lots of seafood.

Vincents $$$ *Jalan Raya Canggu, tel: 0363-41368.* Open daily for lunch and dinner. Vincents offers good quality international and local cuisine with plenty of vegetarian options.

NORTHERN BALI

LOVINA

Damai Restaurant $$$$$ *Jalan Damai, Lovina, tel: 0362-41008.* Open daily for lunch and dinner. On a hill overlooking Lovina, with sweeping vistas, this restaurant serves exquisite 'nouvelle Indonesian' cuisine. Each plate is a visual and gustatory work of art. Free shuttle to Lovina hotels. Major credit cards.

Warung Kopi Bali $ *Jalan Bina Ria, Lovina Beach, tel: 0362-41361.* Open daily 7am–11pm. The most congenial of the downtown eating places, offering seafood, pizza, Chinese and Balinese choices, plus 7pm–9pm happy hour deals on drinks. Cash only.

LOMBOK

Asmara Restaurant $$ *Jalan Raya Senggigi, tel: 0370-693 619.* A lovely place with consistently good international and local food.

Lotus Restaurant $$$ *Art Markets, Senggigi Beach, tel: 0370-693 758.* Good quality Italian food in a beachfront setting.

Tropicana Grand Café $$$ *Jalan Raya Senggigi, tel: 0370-693 432.* A popular gathering place for both dancing and dining.

A–Z TRAVEL TIPS

A Summary of Practical Information

A

ACCOMMODATION (See also YOUTH HOSTELS on page 132)

'Bali Style', a mixture of Western amenities, lavish tropical surroundings, Balinese architecture, understated, open-air design and harmonious aesthetics, has become world famous. You'll find hotels in every price range that blend various proportions of Bali Style with special grace and charm. A growing number of exclusive luxury villas in Bali's most breathtaking locations offer private accommodation that is magical, as well as personal pampering. Additionally, there are villa complexes, operated as hotels, with private facilities and a 5-star standard of service. There are also many large international hotels in a similar high-price bracket, all planned to provide at least a touch of special Balinese ambiance. Somewhat less expensive are the 2-, 3- and 4-star hotels designed mainly for the package tour business and concentrated in the resort areas. These are comfortable, mildly exotic and often available at discounts as part of tour packages or through agents that specialise in travel to Bali. Many smaller hotels in these price ranges are truly personal, unique places – rustic Balinese-style structures in exquisite settings. Balinese hotels are mostly low-rise.

A **losmen** is a small, family-run hotel. The word **homestay** conveys the idea of living with a local family on a room-and-breakfast or room-and-board basis. 'Losmen' and 'homestay' are used interchangeably and can be anything from a small beach resort to a traditional family compound with a room to rent. The owners are used to showing rooms to prospective clients and bargaining over prices.

Rates quoted are generally for room only. More modest places often include a basic breakfast. In standard hotels, breakfast is often extra. There is only a small difference (or none) between rates for single or double occupancy.

All hotels (but not all losmen) add 10 percent tax and a 10 percent service charge to the bill, compounded to 21 percent. Usually this is not included in the quoted rates.

Lombok has far fewer visitors than Bali, most of whom stay around Senggigi. There are a few tourist hotels around Kuta Beach, on the southern coast. The Gilis offer middle-range, comfortable hotels, *losmen* and, increasingly, luxury villas and villa resorts.

Do you have any vacancies?	**Apakah ada kamar yang kosong?**
a single/double room	**kamar untuk satu/dua orang**
with bath/shower	**dengan kamar mandi atau/shower**

AIRPORTS

Ngurah Rai Airport, Denpasar (code DPS), is 10km (6 miles) from Denpasar. For domestic flights, tel: 0361-751 011, extension 3109; for international flights, tel: 0361-751 011, ext. 1454. Some hotels operate shuttle buses and other minibus services to and from all parts of Bali. Taxis are arranged by a central desk where you exit the terminal. Prices are fixed and payable in advance. The airport has a 24-hour currency exchange and duty-free shops. A departure tax of Rp. 150,000 is payable in cash after check-in for international flights. Domestic flight tax is Rp. 30,000.

Selaparang Airport, Lombok (code AMI), is 1.5km (1 mile) from Mataram and about 12km (7 miles) from the resort area of Senggigi. The only international flights landing at Selaparang Airport are to and from Singapore with Silk Air.

B

BICYCLE AND MOTORCYCLE RENTAL

Bicycles are a favourite local means of travel and a good way to explore country roads in a quiet way. Plenty of **bicycles** are available to rent; rates can be as low as Rp. 40,000 (US$4) per day for a decent bike. Your hotel may rent bicycles or recommend a place to rent from. Insist on a modern mountain bike. You will appreciate its low gears on the steep hills and its shock-absorbing tyres; the minor roads and paths are often rough. Check the condition of spokes, tyres and brakes. You'll need a bell that works and, ideally, reflectors (riding at night is not advised). In case of a puncture or breakdown, wheel your bike to the repair shop that you'll find in almost every village.

Don't consider renting a **motorcycle** unless you are an experienced rider. The unpredictable habits of other road users, including livestock, and the rough surfaces and potholes call for skilful handling. You need an international licence, valid for a motorcycle. Some of the machines for rent may be the property of one person and the agreement may be informal, with doubtful insurance coverage. You might have to hand over your passport as a deposit and pay in advance. Check the condition of the machine before accepting it.

C

CAR RENTAL (*sewa mobil*; see also DRIVING on page 118)

Car rental is easily arranged through the many local companies. Signs offering vehicles for rent are put up by offices that merely pass you on to another company – and collect a commission. Rates at local Balinese agencies are far lower than at the few international companies. Prices (per day) at the local agencies range from Rp. 100,000 (US$10) to Rp. 300,000 (US$30). These rates should include collision insurance, unlimited mileage and pick-up and delivery service. Petrol is not included in the price. To rent a self-drive vehicle, you must have a valid Indonesian or International Driving Licence. Payment in advance for the whole rental period is often expected. Some companies accept major credit cards. Always bargain. You can often get a lower price for longer rental periods, or if demand is slack. Compare several agencies if possible.

A Jeep-type vehicle with high ground clearance is essential if you intend to get off the busy main roads.

The condition and functioning of rental cars varies greatly, so take a test drive and check everything (wipers, horn, spare tyre, lights) before accepting the vehicle. Make sure that all damage is recorded.

Insurance. Very limited insurance is mandatory. The better companies have agreements with big insurers and will issue a policy document. Others are more casual, assuring you that minimal insurance is 'included'. Try to get written evidence of just what is covered. Check all wording before signing the rental agreement.

If rental difficulties and driving conditions (see DRIVING, page 118) put you off, rent a **car with a driver** for half a day (about Rp. 200,000) or a full day (Rp. 350,000). He will be responsible for the vehicle, dealing with problems, and will probably act as guide and interpreter. Don't forget to give him money for meals. Travel agencies (see GUIDES AND TOURS, page 120) can arrange for cars with drivers at very reasonable rates; touts on the streets of main tourist centres can supply cars and drivers for even lower prices. Ask other tourists or your hotel for recommended drivers. Some are quite good.

CLIMATE AND CLOTHING (*pakaian*)

This close to the equator, temperatures remain stable year-round. In lowland areas, they range from a nightly minimum of 24°C (75°F) to an average daily high of 32°C (89°F) in the shade. Mountain areas can be a lot cooler. The rainy season runs from December to March, although most days will see some sunshine. It's dry from June to September, and intermediate months are changeable. Humidity is high at all times of the year.

Clothing. Travel light. You'll rarely need anything more than the most casual summer clothes, and Bali is a good place to buy casual and beachwear inexpensively. The local sarong can be a useful accessory for men as well as women. Brief or revealing dress is only acceptable in resort centres. On visits to religious sites, anyone wearing shorts, a tank top or bikini top will offend locals and probably won't be allowed in, although at many temples you can solve the problem by renting a sarong. It's also advisable to dress respectably when visiting government offices. Long sleeves and a hat are recommended whenever you are likely to be out in the sun for any length of time. Out of doors in the evenings, protect arms and legs against mosquitoes. It can be much cooler in the hills, and if you plan an expedition to the mountains prepare for it to be chilly at night.

Indonesians are quite fashion-conscious, and many visitors in the resort hotels also like to dress up in the evening. A *batik* or white shirt is standard semi-formal wear for men.

Remember to take the following as it might be time-consuming to find them locally: sunblock, sunglasses and sun hat, earplugs (dogs bark all night in villages and cocks crow long before dawn), rubber footwear for coral beaches and reefs, and mosquito repellent.

CRIME (See also EMERGENCIES on page 119 and POLICE on page 128)

Take commonsense precautions and be on your guard. Put valuables in your hotel safe and don't leave any desirable items unguarded while you go for a swim. Watch out for pickpockets, especially in crowded places and on *bemos* and other public transport.

Muggings are almost unheard of, but there have been cases of bag-snatching. Don't wear expensive-looking jewellery and carry only the cash you need. If you do have something of value stolen, you will need to report the loss to a police station to obtain a document to show your insurance company.

The possession, sale, import and export of narcotic drugs is illegal and punished by severe jail sentences or death. Anyone offering you drugs is quite likely to be an informer.

My ticket/wallet/passport has been stolen.	**Tiket/dompet/paspor saya dicuri.**

CUSTOMS *(pabean)*

Weapons, narcotics and pornography are prohibited. If you are carrying medication that might be mistaken for an illegal drug, bring a letter from your doctor or copy of a prescription.

Import or export of more than Rp. 10 million is prohibited. There is no restriction on foreign currency and travellers' cheques. A maximum of 1 litre of alcohol, 200 cigarettes of 50 cigars or 100g of tobacco may be brought into Indonesia. Contact **Airport Customs** (tel: 0361-751 037) for more information.

D

DRIVING *(mengendarai;* see also Car Rental on page 115)

Balinese driving conditions can be chaotic. Nominally, traffic must keep to the left. In southern Bali, roads are often choked with motorbikes balancing three or four passengers as well as chickens, babies and other cargo, while weaving between larger vehicles. One-way streets in towns take you far off your planned route, and parts of the main road network can often seem like one continuous, densely populated village street. Elsewhere, especially north of Klungkung or Mengwi, there's much less traffic and driving becomes a pleasure.

Most major roads are well-surfaced, but in remote regions they can be rough and tortuous. Signs are few and far between. Always carry your driving licence. In towns, the speed limit is 30kph; on highways, 60–80kph. It is legal to make a left turn with caution on a red light.

Fuel and oil. Petrol (gasoline) is available in the grade needed by most rental vehicles: pumps are marked 'Premium'. Filling stations are confined to the main towns, but most villages have a dealer with drums or bottles of fuel *(bensin)* who will measure out the amount you want. The price is slightly more. Look for the sign 'Premium' (sometimes 'Permium') or, on Lombok, a red drum and funnel. Diesel pumps are marked SOLAR. Fuel prices are very low by Western standards. 'Premium' is Rp. 4,500 per litre.

International Driving Permit	**Surat Ijin Mengemudi (SIM) Internasional**
Car registration papers	**Surat Tanda Nomor kendaraan (STNK)**
Where's the nearest petrol station?	**Dimana pom bensin terdekat?**
Full tank, please.	**Tolong diisi penuh.**
Check the oil/tyres/ battery, please.	**Tolong periksa olinya/ban/aki.**
My car has broken down.	**Mobil saya mogok.**

E

ELECTRICITY *(listrik)*

Most hotels are on 220-volt, 50-cycle supply and use plugs with two rounded pins. A few are on 110 volts. Bring your own adaptors.

EMBASSIES *(kedutaan besar)* AND CONSULATES

Australia is the only English-speaking country to have a full-fledged consulate in Bali, at: Jalan Hayam Wuruk 88B, Denpasar, tel: 0361-241 118. Some Canadian and New Zealand affairs can be handled at this office There's a US consular agent at Jalan Hayam Wuruk 188, Denpasar, tel: 0361-233 605 and a British Honorary Consul in Sanur, tel: 0361-270 601. Embassies are in Jakarta.

EMERGENCIES *(darurat)*

The following telephone numbers may be useful:

Emergency Response Centre	112
Police	110
Fire brigade	113
Ambulance	118
Search and Rescue	111/115/151

G

GAY AND LESBIAN TRAVELLERS

Family influence is so strong that local people are all expected to get married eventually. Meanwhile, private liaisons – if they're discreet – are one's own affair. The same attitude applies to the sexual orientation of visitors. Public displays of affection are severely frowned upon (especially in Lombok). Gay-friendly night spots are located in Ji Abimanyu (Dhyana Pura), in Seminyak.

GETTING TO BALI

By Air. Many international airlines fly to Denpasar direct. Competitive prices are widely advertised. Book early if travelling at peak season (July–September and around Christmas).

International flights to Lombok generally involve changing planes at Singapore or Denpasar.

To Bali: Foreign airlines serving Bali include: AirAsia, Cathay Pacific, China Airlines, EVA Air, Japan Airlines, Jetstar Airways, Korean Air, Malaysia Airlines, Qatar Airways, Singapore Airlines and Thai Airways. Flights from the US, Europe and New Zealand involve changing planes in the home country of the airline.

From Java and Lombok: Daily air services are available between Bali and Lombok, and Bali and major cities in Java. A daily ferry service serves Bali and Java, and a ferry goes between Bali and Lombok every two hours. Several companies offer a daily fast boat service between Bali and Lombok.

GUIDES (pengantar) AND TOURS

Organised tours or private cars with drivers and/or guides are good ways to see the major sites in Bali. Local travel agencies can arrange guided itineraries, reserve hotel rooms (often at discounted prices) and arrange travel by plane or ferry to Lombok or other islands. They can also arrange day or overnight guided excursions to the Hindu and Buddhist temple complexes at Prambanan and Borobudur on Java, near the city of Yogyakarta. **Pacto Travel Agency** (tel: 0361-288 449; offices in Sanur and at the Inna Grand Bali Beach Hotel in Sanur) is one of the island's oldest and most reliable agencies. Reputable **Bali Discovery Tours** with its office at Sanur (tel: 0361-286 283; www.balidiscovery.com) can arrange everything from hotels and tours to ground transport. **Bidy Tour** in Lombok (tel: 0370-632 127; www.bidytour-lombok.com) is a solid, reputable company. Another well-reputed tour agency, **Perama Tours** (tel: 0370-693 007 in Lombok, 0361-751 551 in Bali; www.peramatour.com), offers a range of tours and transfers around Lombok and throughout Indonesia.

On an organised tour, guides are provided. Otherwise, you can hire one on the spot when you visit major sites of interest. On the streets of Ubud, Kuta and Sanur, you'll pass endless young men offering 'Transport? Transport?' and miming the act of steering a car. Some travellers negotiate for an excursion with a tout who seems amiable and if that works out, arrange for something longer. Many hotels have tour desks offering excursions. Prices are generally higher than at local agencies; ask fellow travellers for feedback on tours and guides.

Advance planning is essential if you want good prices, a personally tailored itinerary with hotels, resorts and country inns that offer the best of 'Bali Style' and spirit, or if you want to pursue special interests in crafts, sports, nature treks, Balinese art, yoga and meditation, shopping or cuisine. Look into consolidators such as **Travel 2** (in the UK: www.travel2.com) or **Travel Mood** (in the UK: www.travelmood.com).

H

HEALTH AND MEDICAL CARE

Phone 118 for an **ambulance**; a taxi can often get you to the nearest emergency room faster. Foreigners receive routine or emergency medical attention, as well as help with evacuation, at: **International**

SOS Clinic, Jalan Bypass Ngurah Rai 505X, Kuta, tel: 0361-710 505; and **Bali International Medical Centre**, Jalan Ngurah Rai 100X at the Kuta-Sanur-Nusa Dua roundabout, tel: 0361-761 263). Medical staff in hospital emergency rooms will speak English.

Do not drink tap water in Bali or Lombok. Bottled water is inexpensive and readily available. Because of the heat and humidity, drink at least four litres a day to avoid dehydration.

Monosodium Glutamate (MSG), known locally as *vetsin*, is used very heavily in many local Indonesian restaurants. If you have high blood pressure, or are allergic to MSG, keep to simple grilled meats or fish without sauces, and fresh fruits and salads. Always specify that you want food without MSG: *tanpa vetsin*.

Well before leaving home, check with your doctor about any **immunisations** (vaccinations) that may be required. Polio and tetanus shots should be up-to-date. **Malaria** is no longer a threat in Bali, but check as to whether precautions should be taken if you plan to travel to southern Lombok or to the Gilis, especially in the rainy season.

Pharmacies *(apotik)* are quite well stocked.

Medical services must be paid for in cash. Be sure to take out travel insurance, including medical expenses.

Jet Lag. Doctors recommend that visitors eat lightly at first, drink plenty of (non-alcoholic) liquids, and get plenty of rest. Jet lag may only set in on the second day. Staying outdoors helps you adjust to the sunlight and time of day in a new time zone.

For traveller's diarrhea, drink plenty of liquids, get lots of rest, and eat lightly – the problem should go away in a day or two. Many people find a diet of plain rice, bananas and tea to be effective. If you have more serious symptoms, including vomiting, get medical advice.

Wear a sunscreen with high protection factors (SPF 30 or more). Stay out of direct sunlight between 11am and 2pm.

Shower at least twice a day and ideally, whenever you come in from the street, beach or a tour. Thongs (flip-flops) make good indoor footwear; in small hotels or *losmen* wear them in the bathroom and shower. In the simplest accommodation, the bathroom may contain a waist-high tub of water *(bak mandi)* for bathing, and a dipper. Throw water over yourself, soap and rinse. Don't get in the tub!

Dangerous animals. There are several species of poisonous snakes on Bali and Lombok, so avoid walking through vegetation at night. If someone is bitten, keep them as still as possible and transport them to a hospital right away. Bali's dogs look fierce and mangy but they are unlikely to bother you. Rabies is current in Bali.

Intestinal worms are common; some types enter through the soles of the feet, so only go barefoot indoors.

HOLIDAYS

The following are national holidays observed in Indonesia. Public offices and banks close, but shops, especially in tourist areas, will usually be open. In addition to the few holidays listed below, many Islamic, Buddhist, Hindu and some Christian holidays are observed.

1 January	New Year's Day
17 August	Independence Day
25 December	Christmas Day

Nyepi, or Hindu New Year's Day, falls in March or April. From dawn on Nyepi until dawn the next day, **no-one can be outdoors anywhere on the island of Bali**. Tourists are included in this total ban, although guests at hotels with private gardens that are secluded from public view can sometimes use the hotel grounds.

L

LANGUAGE *(bahasa)*

Most Balinese you encounter in hotels, shops and restaurants will know some English. The national language is Bahasa Indonesia, understood by most people although among themselves the Balinese speak their own language.

Three useful Bahasa Indonesia phrases to know are:

Terima kasih	thank you
Hati-hati	careful, be careful
Pelan-pelan	slowly, slow down

In addition to the words listed below, we would recommend the Berlitz *Indonesian Phrase Book and Dictionary*.

banjar	local community (area or council)
bapak	father, term of polite address to older man
bemo	minibus operating as public transport
bukit	hill
desa	village
dokar	pony cart
gang	alleyway, path
gili	island
gunung	mountain
ibu	mother, term of polite address to a lady
ikat (endek)	cloth (threads are pattern-dyed before weaving)
jalan	street, road (jalan jalan = walk, go)
kaja	in the direction of the mountains
klod (kelod)	in the direction of the sea
(bak mandi)	tank of water for bathing (by filling a dipper and pouring water over yourself)
nusa	island
pantai	beach
pasar	market
prahu	outrigger sailing or motorised boat
pura	Hindu temple
puri	palace

Vowels are pronounced:

a like ah, but shorter	**u** as in food
e as in met	**ai** as in like
i as in meet (open),	**au** as in cow
as in sit (closed)	**o** as in go

Consonants generally are pronounced as in English, with the following exceptions:

c as in chin	k at the end of a word is almost silent
g as in guest	r is well-rolled

Emphasis is on the second to the last syllable of a word.

Numbers

1	satu	11	sebelas
2	dua	12	duabelas
3	tiga	20	duapuluh
4	empat	21	duapuluh satu
5	lima	30	tigapuluh
6	enam	100	seratus
7	tujuh	200	dua ratus
8	delapan	1000	seribu
9	sembilan	2000	dua ribu
10	sepuluh	1,000,000	juta

LAUNDRY *(cucian)* AND DRY CLEANING

Many hotels have same-day or next-day laundry and dry-cleaning services, at a price plus 21 percent hotel service and tax. Smaller places may be harder on the clothes and lack the means of thorough drying in rainy weather, but charges are less than Rp. 3.000 per item.

LOST PROPERTY *(barang hilang)*

If loss or suspected theft occurs in your hotel, check first at the reception desk. They may suggest that you report the incident to the police.

This may be time-consuming but necessary for any insurance claim. For something lost elsewhere, try retracing your steps.

M

MEDIA

Newspapers (*surat kabar*) and **magazines** (*majalah*). *The Jakarta Post* is a quality daily newspaper published in Jakarta in English; it reaches Bali the same day. Major resort hotels have the Singapore-printed *Asian Wall Street Journal* and *International Herald Tribune* and several Australian papers by the same evening or next morning. *Bali & Beyond*, *Hello Bali* and *Now Bali* magazines are worthwhile and available free in many hotels. They contain useful information, although their articles and recommendations favour their advertisers.

   Radio (*radio*) and **TV** (*televisi*). Local channels rarely broadcast programs in English, but larger hotels have satellite TV, with CNN, CNBC, the BBC, and Australian news channels. Radio Australia, BBC World Service and Voice of America are well received on short wave.

MONEY MATTERS

Currency. The Indonesian rupiah (Rp or IDR) comes in banknotes (bills) of Rp. 1,000, 2,000, 5,000, 10,000, 20,000, 50,000 and 100,000. There are 50, 100, 200 and 500 rupiah coins.

   Banks and Currency Exchange. Banks are open from 8 or 8.30am to 3pm, Monday–Friday. Moneychangers keep longer hours. Denpasar airport's currency-exchange office is open round the clock, but charges commission. **ATMs** linked to Cirrus and other international systems are available in major towns all over the island. They dispense rupiah. Rates are slightly better than elsewhere. Note that ATMs can run out of money; especially at weekends. Hotels may exchange foreign currency but at unfavourable rates. Moneychangers usually give good rates. Moneychangers are adept in ways to shortchange clients, so do your own calculations and count money carefully. At the time of press, US$1 was equivalent to Rp. 9,250.

Alert your bank and credit card company to the fact that you will be travelling in Indonesia and try to monitor charges against your account by Internet. Card numbers are sometimes copied from sales receipts and used to make **counterfeit ATM and credit cards**, which are then used on wild spending sprees.

Credit Cards. All but the least expensive hotels accept major credit cards, as do some restaurants, shops and car-rental companies, although they may add 3–5 percent to prices to cover the commission they will have to pay. You may be asked for your passport as extra identification. Some banks and big moneychangers will advance cash against a credit card, but they'll take a 4–8 percent commission.

Travellers' Cheques. Hotels, tour operators and many shops and restaurants will accept travellers' cheques in major currencies and they can also be changed at banks and moneychangers. It is a good idea to have some in case of theft or when ATMs are down.

I want to change some pounds/dollars	Saya mau menukar pound sterling/dollar.
Do you accept travellers' cheques?	Boleh dibayar dengan traveller cek?

○

OPENING HOURS (See also Holidays on page 123)

Most **shops** are open from 9am–7pm or 9pm every day; some close on Sunday. **Businesses** may open from 8am–4pm or 9am–5pm, Monday–Friday. **Government offices** operate from 8am–2pm Monday–Thursday and from 8–11.30am Friday.

Government museums (including Le Mayeur Museum in Sanur) are open from 8am–2pm, Tuesday–Sunday. Neka Art Museum and Museum Puri Lukisan in Ubud are open 9am–5pm daily.

P

POLICE *(polisi)*

Regular police wear brown uniforms with a badge showing their name and number. Traffic police have a white or green cap and drive both marked and unmarked vehicles.

Personnel are normally polite and friendly but matters move slowly and bureaucratically in police offices.

POST OFFICES *(kantor pos)*

Open hours Mon–Thur 8am–2pm, Fri 8am–11am, Sat 8am–12.30pm. Post offices are usually crowded, and Denpasar's is not central, in Jalan Raya Puputan, Renon. It's more convenient to buy stamps at postal agencies *(agen pos)* run by many small shops, or at the larger hotels, even if you are not staying there. Important mail should be registered.

airmail/registered	**pos udara/pos tercatat**
A stamp for this letter/ postcard, please.	**Minta membeli prangko untuk surat/kartu pos ini.**

PUBLIC TRANSPORT

Buses *(bis)*. Cheap but generally overcrowded. Budget travellers use the buses that connect with ferries to Java and Lombok.

Tourist Buses. Usually vans that offer shuttle service between the major tourist destinations. Fares are higher than local public buses but very reasonable by Western standards. If you are travelling in a group of 3 or 4, it might prove more cost-effective to charter a *bemo*.

Bemos. Minivans follow a fixed route, picking up and setting down passengers, and some are painted according to their usual destination – try to get to know the colours. Prices are fixed but you will be overcharged unless you know the right fare. Ask at your hotel about *bemo* routes and fares and watch what others pay.

Taxis *(taksi)*. There are supposed to be fixed official rates for all journeys but many drivers will try for a higher fare. Check with your hotel for the approximate rate to a destination and always agree on the fare in advance unless there is a meter. Even if taxis have meters, drivers try to avoid using them or persuade you that they have the right to charge much more. Insist that meters are switched on.

Dokar or Andong. Tiny ponies pull two-wheeled carts, often laden with passengers or sacks of rice. Decide fares before boarding. In Lombok, a *cidomo* is similar, but with car tyres.

Ferries *(ferry)*. Car and passenger ferry services connect Gilimanuk in west Bali with Java, and Padangbai in east Bali with Lembar, Lombok. In addition, small boats sail to the offshore islands on demand, if anyone is prepared to pay.

Fast boats. A number of fast boat services connect Bali to Nusa Lembongan Island, Lombok and Gili Trawangan.

Inter-island Flights. Various local airlines operate many times a day from Denpasar to Mataram, Lombok – it's virtually a shuttle service. Both islands are also connected frequently to their neighbours and thus to all main centres in Indonesia.

R

RELIGION *(agama)*

The Balinese follow their special form of Hinduism. Most people in Lombok are Muslim, with a substantial Bali-Hindu minority on the western coast. Ask at the front desk of your hotel for times and locations of Christian churches.

T

TELEPHONES *(telepon)*

When calling Indonesia from abroad, use the country code (62), followed by the area code (omitting the initial 0) and the local number. The Bali area codes are 0361 (Denpasar, Gianyar, Kuta, Nusa Dua, Sanur, Tabanan, Ubud); 0362 (Buleleng, Lovina, Singaraja); 0363 (Candidasa, Karangasem), 0365 (Jembrana, Negara), 0366 (Bangli, Klungkung), 0368 (Bedugul); and 0370 (Lombok).

For international calls *from* Indonesia, dial 001 or 007, the country code, the area code (omitting the initial 0) and the local number. For an **international operator, dial 102**.

Hotels add extra charges, sometimes large ones, to telephone calls. You may do better by using one of the calling cards issued by international telephone companies (hotels then charge only for a local call).

At the highly efficient **WARTEL offices**, found in most towns and resort areas, you can make local and international calls, both economically and without delay.

Mobile phones. These can be used in Bali if they operate on the GSM network. Prepaid phone cards are available for mobile phones. You will get a local number beginning with 08.

TIME DIFFERENCES

Bali and Lombok are on GMT (UTC) + 8 hours.

New York	London	Jo'burg	**Bali**	Sydney	Auckland
11pm	4am	6am	**noon**	2pm	4pm

TIPPING

A service charge of 10 percent is added to most hotel and some restaurant bills, but tipping is not expected in small local eating places. It's appropriate to give a small tip to porters for their services.

The table below gives some suggestions as to how much to leave.

Taxi drivers	Rp. 5,000–10,000
Personal drivers and guides	10 percent
Porters	Rp. 2,000–5,000 per bag

TOILETS *(kamar kecil, WC)*

All hotels intended for Western visitors have Western-style facilities. Elsewhere they are likely to be simpler, and in rural areas rudimentary or nonexistent. Carry your own paper when travelling around the islands. Where there are no flush toilets, use the dipper and tub of water provided for flushing.

TOURIST INFORMATION OFFICES *(kantor turis)*

Local offices have little printed material but may be able to tell you about the venues, dates and times of events and ceremonies.

Denpasar: Bali Government Tourism Office, Jalan Supratman, Niti Mandala Renon, tel: 0361-222 387. Unfortunately located far from any tourist area, this office has a few pamphlets and information on events and performances in Bali.

Ubud: There is an information stand, Bina Wisata, in Jalan Raya Ubud, opposite the Ubud Palace, tel: 0361-973 285. This is probably the best tourism office in Bali.

Mataram, Lombok: Jalan Langko 70, tel: 0370-631 730. Useful maps and information, but frequently out of stock.

TRAVELLERS WITH DISABILITIES

Only the most modern hotels have rooms that cater to the needs of travellers with disabilities. Many hotels are spread out, sometimes on hilly, stepped sites. Temples include many steps; city and village sidewalks are littered with hazards and obstacles. Entering almost every shop, restaurant and hotel entails climbing up and down threshold steps. Staircases, both indoor and outdoor, are built with dangerously uneven steps and treads.

V

VISAS

Citizens of more than 60 countries, including Australia, New Zealand, the UK and the United States, will be granted a visa on arrival for a fee of US$25 for 30 days. Visitors from most other countries must obtain a 30-day tourist visa from their local Indonesian consulate or embassy. Anyone wishing to stay longer than 30 days must apply for a visa overseas at an Indonesian embassy or consulate before travelling. Your passport must be valid for six months upon entry into Indonesia, and you must also have a confirmed ticket for passage out of the country.

W

WEBSITES

Bali Online www.indo.com – festivals, history and culture.
Bali Paradise www.baliparadise.com – hotel information, bookings, diving, sailing and other activities and upcoming festivals.
Private Homes & Villas www.phvillas.com – villa rental agency.
Bali Discovery www.balidiscovery.com – tour operator which can book accommodation, tours, activities, ground transportation, etc.
Bali Travel Forum www.balitravelforum.com – contains an interesting section on comments and experiences by other travellers.
US State Department Consular Information Site www.us embassyjakarta.org – a good place to check about current political conditions and travel advisories throughout Indonesia.

Y

YOUTH HOSTELS

A few simple homestays call themselves hostels and some offer dormitory-style rooms with up to four beds.

Recommended Hotels

The hotels below are listed by geographical area. The rates given are for a double room with private bath or shower, not including breakfast. Service and tax, totalling 21 percent, are additional. Room rates can be considerably lower as part of an inclusive package, and low-season discounts may be available. The busiest times are from July to September and from Christmas to late January. If you plan to visit then, make reservations well in advance. Rooms have air-conditioning unless otherwise stated, with most exceptions in the mountains, where it is unneccessary. Hotels in the larger towns are used mainly by local business travellers and probably won't appeal to holiday visitors. Hotels accept major credit cards unless otherwise noted.

You can also find simpler kinds of budget accommodation *(see page 113)* that can cost a fraction of the lowest price quoted here.

$$$$$	over $250
$$$$	$140–250
$$$	$70–140
$$	$30–70
$	up to $30

SOUTHERN BALI

DENPASAR

Inna Bali $$ *Jalan Veteran 3, tel: 0361-225 681, fax: 0361-235 347.* Central, near Puputan Square, with a garden and pool. Built in the colonial era, it was once the only hotel in Bali. A more modern annex has been added across the street. Rooms are comfortable. 80 rooms.

JIMBARAN BEACH

Ayana Resort & Spa $$$$$ *Jalan Karang Mas Sejahtera, tel: 0361-702 222, fax 0361-701 555, www.ayanaresort.com.* This resort comprises 78 freestanding villas and a 290-room hotel. The 12 dining venues include Rock Bar, which is located on natural rocks above the ocean. One of five swimming pools, the Ocean Beach Pool extends from the base of the cliff overlooking the white-sand beach. Lovely wedding pavilions and luxurious spa facilities complete the picture.

Bali Inter-Continental $$$$$ *Jalan Uluwatu 45, tel: 0361-701 888, fax: 0361-701 777, http://bali.intercontinental.com.* Set in 14 hectares (35 acres) of extensive landscaped gardens and lagoons, this resort has a beautiful beach and is in an ideal spot for viewing sunsets. Squash and tennis courts, a spa, three swimming pools, a health club, water sports facilities and bars on the premises. 425 rooms.

Four Seasons Resort Bali at Jimbaran Bay $$$$$+ *Jimbaran, tel: 0361-701 010, fax: 0361-701 020, www.fourseasons.com.* Designed to suggest a Balinese village on a hillside overlooking Jimbaran Bay, this is one of the most architecturally acclaimed luxury resorts in the world. Each room is a spacious, beautifully decorated villa with walled garden, outdoor shower and plunge pool. Stairs lead down to the sandy beach and watersports centre. 147 rooms.

Ritz-Carlton $$$$$ *Jalan Karang Mas Sejahtera, tel: 0361-702 222, fax: 0361-701 555, www.ritzcarlton.com.* An award-winning four-storey resort with dramatic views of the Indian Ocean. It is entirely self-contained, with a large pool, 18-hole golf putting course, tennis courts, kids' club, gym, sauna, nursery, spa complex and five restaurants on the premises. Access to the beach, however, is via a staircase down a steep slope. 322 rooms.

KUTA BEACH

Alam KulKul $$$ *Jalan Pantai Kuta, tel: 0361-752 520, fax: 0361-752 519, www.alamkulkul.com.* Just across the road from Kuta Beach, this chic resort offers a choice of luxurious rooms and small private villas set among lovely old banyan trees. It also incorporates the Jamu Spa, a kids' daycare centre, an Indonesian specialty restaurant and Papa's Restaurant serving Italian cuisine.

Hard Rock Hotel $$$$ *Jalan Pantai Banjar Pande Mas, tel: 0361-761 869, fax: 0361-761 868, www.hardrockhotels.net.* An up-to-the-minute world of shops, pubs, restaurants and discos attached to four vast floors of guest rooms, each floor representing a different era of music from the 1950s to the 1990s. Gigantic swimming pool; nightly concerts and performances. 418 rooms.

Poppies Cottages $$–$$$ *off Poppies Gang, tel: 0361-751 059, fax: 0361-752 364, www.poppies.com.* Down a motorbike-filled alley, you'll find this Kuta institution, hidden in a walled garden. Rooms in traditional brick cottages have been upgraded and have fridges but no TVs. Swimming pool, air-conditioning and location at centre of the Kuta scene are pluses. Walk to beach. 20 rooms.

LEGIAN BEACH

Legian Beach Hotel $$$$ *Jalan Melasti, tel: 0361-751 711, fax: 0361-752 652, www.legianbeachbali.com.* Right at the centre of Kuta Bay, on a perfect stretch of beach with great waves, this three-star resort is an easy walk to restaurants, markets and nightlife. Pleasant grounds; extra large fountain-lined pool and spa. Rooms are small and furnished simply; those in the garden bungalows are worth the extra price. 217 rooms.

Padma Resort Bali at Legian $$$$ *Jalan Padma 1, Legian, tel: 0361-752 111, fax: 0361-752 140; www.padmaresortbali.com.* With 406 comfortable rooms and suites, all with private balconies, this is the largest hotel in the Legian area; it is romantically set amid 6.8 hectares (17 acres) of gardens and has over 200m (650ft) of beachfront. Facilities at the resort include the Padma Spa by Mandara, two tennis courts and a fitness centre, a boutique and gallery, and a good choice of restaurants.

SEMINYAK BEACH

The Legian $$$$$ *Jalan Laksmana, Seminyak Beach, tel: 0361-730 622, fax: 0361-73191, www.ghmhotels.com/thelegian.* Over-sized and luxurious sea-facing suites contained within a low-rise property on a broad sandy beach. Top-class beachfront restaurant and spa make this the ideal getaway. 71 suites.

Oberoi Bali \$\$\$\$\$ *Jalan Laksmana, tel: 0361-730 361, fax: 0361-730 791, www.oberoihotels.com*. There are 75 spacious and luxuriously equipped cottages and villas, amid beautiful gardens, north of Legian, next to a huge and uncrowded sandy beach. The Oberoi is highly rated for its design, standards of service and cuisine. There are frequent Balinese dance performances staged in an outdoor theatre.

Sofitel Seminyak Bali \$\$\$\$ *Jalan Camplung Tanduk, Seminyak Beach, tel: 0361-730 730, fax: 0361-730 545, www.sofitel.com*. This sprawling beachside resort combines modern French luxury with Balinese elegance. There are 17 secluded spa villas, each with a private pool. All rooms feature a balcony with impressive garden views, while each of the villas is encircled by green foliage for complete privacy.

NUSA DUA

Amanusa \$\$\$\$\$+ *Nusa Dua, tel: 0361-772 333, fax: 0361-772 335, www.amanresorts.com*. Luxuriously appointed, each of the 35 private villas has its own garden, set on a hilltop next to a golf course overlooking the Nusa Dua resort area. Facilities include a tennis court, large swimming pool, shuttle service to the private beach club and watersports. The restaurant excels in Thai dishes.

Conrad Bali \$\$\$\$\$, *Jalan Pratama, Tanjung Benoa, tel: 0361-778 788, fax: 0361-773 888, www.conradbali.com*. Each of the 360 rooms and suites here has a private patio or balcony offering panoramic views over the ocean, lagoons or gardens. Large swimming pool, lagoon pool, fitness club, restaurants and bars.

Grand Hyatt Bali \$\$\$\$\$ *Nusa Dua, tel: 0361-771 234, fax: 0361-772 038, www.hyatt.com*. One of the most spectacular resorts in Asia, with spacious rooms set in four Balinese-style 'villages'. All have air-conditioning, satellite TV and IDD telephone. There are six swimming pools, restaurants, spa, business centre, fitness centre and various other recreational facilities. 672 rooms.

Laguna Resort & Spa \$\$\$\$\$ *Nusa Dua Beach, tel: 0361-771 327, fax: 0361-771 326, www.starwoodhotels.com*. The vast swimming pool with sand beaches virtually surrounds this luxury resort and its gardens. Higher price rooms let you step from your balcony into the water. Excellent restaurants, beach and every amenity. 276 rooms.

SANUR

Bali Hyatt $$$$–$$$$$ *Jalan Danau Tamblingan 89, tel: 0361-288 271, fax: 0361-287 693, www.bali.hyatt.com.* Balinese architecture and decor; a perfect white sand beach with calm water; and lavish gardens with over 600 plant species all mark this luxury property. Two pools, tennis courts, water sports. 387 rooms.

Sanur Beach $$$$ *Semawang Sanur, Denpasar, tel: 0361-288 011, fax: 0361-287 566, email: sanurbch@dps.mega.net.id.* This big resort hotel faces the southern end of Sanur Beach. Guest rooms are in several interconnecting wings facing the pools or garden courtyards. Tennis and badminton courts, three swimming pools, and a water-sports centre. Thai, seafood and other restaurants. 425 rooms.

UBUD AND VICINITY

Agung Raka Bungalows $$–$$$ *Pengosekan, tel: 0361-975 757, fax: 0361-975 546, email: agungrak@indo.com.* Except for four standard units, each room is a private, beautifully designed interpretation of the traditional two-storey, thatched roof, rustic Balinese house. Higher priced units are set in tranquil, green rice fields; all have luxury garden bathrooms. Swimming pool, free shuttle to Ubud, 3km (2 miles) away. 18 rooms. No AmEx.

Alila Ubud $$$$$ *Melinggih Kelod, Payangan, tel: 0361-975 963, fax: 0361-975 968, www.alilahotels.com.* Atmospheric resort offering mountain, rice-terrace and river-valley views. Stunning green-tiled swimming pool, a fine restaurant and a complete spa with traditional treatments. 64 rooms.

Ananda Cottages $$$ *Campuhan, tel: 0361-975 376, fax: 0361-975 375, email: anandaubud@denpasar.wasantara.net.id.* Bungalows and Balinese pavilions set amid sprawling, natural gardens with streams that lead to a breathtaking panorama of lush rice fields. Wide variety of rooms including new, air-conditioned bungalows and one luxury villa. Two pools; easy-going service. 50 rooms.

Amandari $$$$$+ *Kedewastan, tel: 0361-975 333, fax: 0361-975 335, www.amanresorts.com.* Exquisite luxury suites, each set in its own walled garden, some with upper-storey bedrooms and private pools. The resort is rich with rustic Balinese architectural influences and atmosphere; the helpful staff are knowledgeable about local culture. Large swimming pool and superb restaurant with wonderful views over the Ayung gorge. 30 suites and 1 3-bedroom villa.

Four Seasons Sayan $$$$$+ *Sayan, Ubud, tel: 0361-977 577, fax: 0361-977 588, www.fourseasons.com.* Contemporary architecture blends gracefully into the most dazzling jungle setting imaginable, overlooking the Ayung River gorge. Two-storey suites and villas offer vistas plus luxury amid sleek Balinese and international design. Magical horizon pool; shuttle to Ubud until 3pm. 18 suites, 42 villas.

Ibah $$$$–$$$$$ *Jalan Campuhan, tel: 0361-974 466, fax: 0361-974 467, www.ibahbali.com.* 18 spacious, air-conditioned villas with modern conveniences, set in spacious gardens. Located in the centre of town. Fabulous pool and one of the best restaurants in Ubud.

Pertiwi Bungalows $$$–$$$$$ *Monkey Forest Road, tel: 0361-975 236, fax: 0361-975 599, www.indo.com/hotels/pertiwi.* With a wide variety of rooms ranging from simple to luxury villa, this tranquil hotel, surrounded by Balinese gardens, offers a respite from the busy world of downtown Ubud just outside its walls. Two pools, lots of traditional Balinese decor. 50 rooms. No AmEx.

Hotel Tjampuhan $$–$$$ *Campuhan, tel: 0361-975 368, fax: 0361-975 137.* Rustic buildings house 55 rooms. Cliffside gardens overlooking the Campuhan River gorge contain the house built by artist Walter Spies in the 1930s; the hotel retains the lush jungle ambiance of those days. Two swimming pools (one spring fed); tennis and badminton courts; natural spa; free shuttle to town.

CANDIDASA/BALINA BEACH DISTRICT

Amankila $$$$$+ *Mangis, tel: 0363-41333, fax: 0363-41555, www.amanresorts.com.* Tumbling down a breathtaking terraced cliff by the sea, this villa resort combines sleek, modern luxury with understated touches of Balinese elegance. Infinity-edge pools, private bridges to each luxury villa; gorgeous beach (though tides are prone to pollution). Pampered service, every amenity; shuttle. 34 suites.

The Watergarden $$$$–$$$$$ *Jalan Raya, Candidasa Beach, tel: 0363-41540, fax: 0363-41164, email: watergardn@denpasar. wasantara.net.id.* Light, tropical rooms surrounded by lush gardens and lotus-filled streams and ponds; pool, beach and delightful ambiance. 14 rooms.

PADANGBAI

Rai Beach Inn $ *Jalan Silayukti, tel: 0363-41439.* This inn has 21 rooms in simple but pleasant cottages, not air-conditioned. Each has a cold salt-water shower and freshwater *mandi*. It faces the beach and fishing village, and is close to the port (for the ferry to Lombok). The dining room is one of the best places to eat in Padangbai. Cash only.

NORTHERN BALI

LOVINA

Aneka Lovina Hotel $$ *Lovina Beach, tel: 0362-41121, fax: 0362-41023, email: anklovina@denpasar.wasantara.net.id.* Bright, comfortable rooms with TVs set in gardens leading to a long stretch of dark-sand beach. There's a swimming pool and watersports; windsurfing and other activities can be arranged. 59 rooms. No AmEx.

Angsoka Cottages $ *Lovina Beach, tel: 0362-41268, fax: 0362-41023, email: angsoka@singaraja.wasantara.net.id.* Right on the beach in the very centre of town, this budget favourite offers a variety of simple but adequate rooms with or without air-conditioning. Large swimming pool. 30 rooms. No credit cards.

Damai Lovina Villas $$$$$ *Jalan Damai, Kayuputih, tel: 0362-41008, fax: 0362-41009, www.damai.com*. Luxurious villas set on a mountain slope and surrounded by rice fields, spice plantations and tropical jungle. It's a quiet and peaceful gateway with an excellent restaurant. 8 villas.

Puri Bagus $$$$ *Lovina Beach, tel: 0362-21430, fax: 0362-22627, email: pblovina@denpasar.wasantara.net.id*. Airy, luxury villas in the Balinese/international style spread along the beach. Large pool, pleasant garden, morning shuttles to town.

MOUNTAINS

Pacung Mountain Resort Inn $$$$$ *Bedugul, tel: 0368-221 038, fax: 0368-221 043, email: pacungmr@balipacung.com*. The most expensive accommodation in the Lake Bratan/Lake Buyan area, this hotel (pronounced 'Pachung') offers standard and deluxe rooms, and more charming luxury bungalows, all with lovely vistas. Small pool; the restaurant is a stop for tour groups. 39 rooms.

Puri Lumbung $$ *Munduk, tel: 0362-92810, fax: 0362-92514, email: lumbung@indosat.net.id*. Charming, traditional rice barn-style cottages with vistas over rice terraces in a village west of Lake Tamblingan. Superb area for mountain hikes, cycling and canoeing; also within easy reach of northcoast beaches. Rustic restaurant; exceptional programmes in eco-hikes, village culture and yoga and homestay programme in co-operation with the town of Munduk for under $25 per night. 17 rooms.

Sacred Mountain Sanctuary $$$–$$$$ *Sideman Karangasem, tel: 0366-24330, fax: 0366-23456*. This exquisitely designed eco-resort is located above a jungle river in the foothills of Mt Agung, in eastern Bali. The Sanctuary envelops you in the natural beauty of the island, and guestrooms blend gracefully into the surroundings. Facilities include a 23m (75ft) spring-fed swimming pool, and spirituality, meditation, massage and nature programmes; there are no televisions. The excellent but expensive meals are extra. 19 rooms.

WEST BALI

Gajah Mina Beach Resort $$$–$$$$ *Suraberata, Lalanglinggah, Selemadeg, Tabanan, tel: (mobile) 081 934-355-633, www. gajah-minaresort.com.* This charming hotel offers individual Balinese-style villas, a restaurant and a swimming pool dotted across a dazzling headland above a private beach. The remote location makes it an ideal choice for those looking to escape from the busy tourist areas.

Waka Shorea $$$$–$$$$$ *Bali Barat National Park, tel: (mobile) 082-836 1431, www.wakaexperience.com.* Set in an unspoiled location accessible only by boat, this is one of only a handful of resorts in the vast Barat Bali National Park. New, marvellously designed bungalows and villas blended into surroundings; hikes, snorkelling and other eco-activities; pool and beautiful sandy beach. 14 rooms.

LOMBOK

Bulan Baru New Moon Hotel $ *Four miles north of Senggigi, tel: 0370-693 785, fax: 0370-693 786, email: bulanbaru@hotmail.com.* Comfortable rooms with air-conditioning and mini-bar, set around a pool and garden. Beautiful beach across the road and peaceful, idyllic location. A 7-minute drive into town. 12 rooms; No AmEx.

Senggigi Beach $$$–$$$$ *Jalan Raya, Senggigi, tel: 0370-693 210, fax: 0370-693 339, www.senggigibeachhotel.com.* With lavish gardens and a private, sandy beach, this hotel offers well-equipped, comfortable rooms. Garden villas are more expensive. A full range of watersports is offered. Nightly outdoor dining events and frequent cultural shows are staged. Five-minute walk into town. 150 rooms.

Sheraton Senggigi Beach $$$$ *Sengiggi, tel: 0370-693 333, fax: 0370-693 140, www.sheraton.com/senggigi.* A relaxed, luxurious resort. Tropical-style guest rooms in three-level buildings set among densely shaded gardens beside a sheltered beach. Facilities include tennis courts; swimming pool; watersports centre; health club; and disco. Frequent special dining events and cultural performances. Three-minute walk into town. 154 rooms.

INDEX

Berlitz® pocket guide
Bali & Lombok

Thirteenth Edition 2010
Reprinted 2012

Written by Robert Ullian
Updated by Rachel Lovelock
Series Editor: Tom Stainer

Photography credits
Jon Davison 13, 16, 17, 24, 28, 48, 58, 62, 86, 91,
97; Corrie Wingate 3BR, 4–5 (all) 48, 11, 14,
26, 31, 32, 34, 35, 36, 39, 40, 41, 42, 44, 46, 49,
50, 52, 54, 55, 56, 61, 63, 65, 66, 69, 71, 72, 84,
89, 92, 98, 101, 102, 104, 105; Archives of the
Royal Tropical Institute, Amsterdam 18; Hans
Hoefer 22; Hulton Archive/Getty Images 21;
iStockphoto.com 2BR, 3M, 74, 77, 78, 81, 82, 94

Cover picture: Getty Images

Every effort has been made to provide
accurate information in this publication,
but changes are inevitable. The publisher
cannot be responsible for any resulting
loss, inconvenience or injury.

Contact us

At Berlitz we strive to keep our guides as
accurate and up to date as possible, but if you
find anything that has changed, or if you have
any suggestions on ways to improve this guide,
then we would be delighted to hear from you.

Berlitz Publishing, PO Box 7910,
London SE1 1WE, England.
email: berlitz@apaguide.co.uk
www.berlitzpublishing.com

www.berlitzpublishing.com

BERLITZ PHRASE BOOKS
The Perfect Companion for your Pocket Guides

Speaking Your Language

Available in more than 30 languages, including Mandarin Chinese, Danish, Hindi and Hungarian